POETRY
AS A
Spiritual Practice

ILLUMINATING THE
Awakened Woman

EDITED BY

CATHERINE GHOSH

WITH

SANDRA MARIE ALLAGAPEN, JAMIE BURGESS,

JESSE JAMES AND TAMMY T. STONE

2016

Golden Dragonfly Press

FIRST PRINT EDITION, June 2016
FIRST EBOOK EDITION, June 2016

First published in the United States of America
by Golden Dragonfly Press, 2016.

www.goldendragonflypress.com

Where the wildflower lives,
the joy of perfect stillness.
Where the grass grows tall,
a safe harbor and echo
Divine.
Amid this vast greatness
the gentle un-falling of
our voice, in flight.

Tammy T. Stone

CONTENTS

PART I

Awakening

CHAPTER 1: NEW MOON

CHAPTER 2: WAXING CRESCENT MOON

PART II

Blossoming

Chapter 4: Waxing Gibbous Moon

Chapter 5: Full Moon

Chapter 6: Waning Gibbous Moon

PART III

Integrating

Chapter 7: Last Quarter Moon

Chapter 8: Waning Crescent Moon

"'Tis moonlight, summer moonlight,
All soft and still and fair;
The solemn hour of midnight
Breathes sweet thoughts everywhere..."

Emily Bronte

INTRODUCTION

BY CATHERINE GHOSH

Within every woman, lives a wild and wonderfully awakened woman. Fiercely attuned to nature—and the deep sense of interconnectedness between all living beings—we often find her engaged in dialogue with the windswept trees, the ocean's tides, the scents of spring. Feeling herself one in substance with all of existence, the awakened woman—made of more than just stardust—frequents the unfathomable depths of her own inner cosmos. It is here that she shines with timeless wisdom, power and beauty.

Paradoxically, we also find the awakened woman teetering capriciously on the shadowy edge of being and becoming. For, much like the moon, she conceals and reveals herself, to the intuitive pulse of her own sacred rhythm. Whether shining brightly in darkness, or veiling herself within it, the awakened woman is aware of a deep and persistent calling, that urges her towards creative expression: the sharing of her voice.

Tracing her voice back to oral traditions, we find the light of the awakened woman often emanating as poetry. For the language of poetry, after all, yields to our longing to define the ineffable. Before blazing fires and under full moons, ancient tribes saw that women held the same creative magic in their wombs as that which originated the entire universe. Acting thus as conduits of divinity, the poetic words that flowed from women of our past, became a tribe's main teachers, healers and guides.

The inspired and inspiring words in this book spontaneously revive that ancient paradigm, illuminating a powerful relationship between poetic expression, and spiritual introspection, that still thrives in the minds and hearts of awakening women. Transcending bonds of culture, race, religion and nationality, the unifying force behind the contributors to this anthology, is rooted in the their shared experience of engaging poetry as a spiritual practice. While some seek exodus from traditional religions, and others draw treasures from theirs, the authors of this book each engage poetry in their individual lives, in a meaningful manner that is sacred to them.

Unique in her own ways of doing so, the spiritual poet typically writes, out of irresistible impulse, her poetry often emerging cyclically and without warning. Mirroring women's phases of poetic expression and introspection, the voices in this volume appear in chapters that reflect the phases of the moon.

Whether recording a message from her psyche, the universe, divinity or her own heart, the spiritual poet certainly does not take the process of receiving and writing a poem for granted. For her, poetry can easily resound with the qualities of prayer, meditation, mysticism or revelation. Connecting with her own sense of the sacred, everything the awakened woman experiences becomes a potential seed that may impregnate her fertile spirit with poetry. Sunrises, the sound of an owl, good conversations, inner conflicts, moonlit nights: all spark feelings that she may very well brew into a poem one day. The awakened woman then gives her words wings by releasing them into flight through books such as the one you now hold in your hands: casting an evanescent light on her secrets, and, in doing so, hoping to inspire other women to do the same.

"This is a call for women
to know and believe in the holiness of their bodies,
the sacredness in their dance,
and the power in their voice."

ZOLA DUBNIKOVA

ACKNOWLEDGEMENTS

This book emerged online from the combined vision and effort of 23 key members of the *Journey of the Heart Poetry Project*: a virtual community founded in 2012 consisting of hundreds of women from all over the world dedicated to spiritually supporting, inspiring and empowering one another by releasing their voices through poetry.

Were it not for the diligent team-effort of six of the authors—who generously volunteered to serve in the book production team as "midwives"—this project would have not been birthed as smoothly and swiftly as it was. Together, they blew fresh breezes into my sails when I needed it most, and happily offered many of their wonderful skills to the project. Therefore, my heart felt gratitude extends first to them:

I am grateful to Kim Buskala and Julia W. Prentice whose eagerness to join the book production team was much appreciated, as was their overall supportive spirit and occasional input in making important miscellaneous decisions. Kim wrote the introduction to chapter six, on the waning gibbous moon, and Julia wrote the introduction to the book's first new moon chapter.

I offer special thanks to Sandra Allagapen for the delicate care she gave the organizing of material, placing content into chapters, helping me retrieve chapter introductions, and especially for her characteristically enthusiastic spirit, which always makes her a pleasure to work with.

Many thanks to our most thorough and meticulous editor, Jamie Burgess, whose attention to commas, hyphens, extra spaces, and ill constructed grammar is much appreciated.

Jamie also contributed the book's climactic chapter introduction on the full moon, and served as the manuscript's final proof reader at the last minute.

Tammy T. Stone's swift responsiveness and thematic sensitivity to submitted material helped me tremendously when making difficult and sweeping editorial adjustments. She assisted in editing all the personal essays and worked with individual authors on their pieces to enhance content flow. Tammy also wrote the introduction to chapter eight on the waning crescent moon, and energized me with her peaceful personality and her efficient work rhythm.

My last words of appreciation for the individual members on this special team of "midwives" go to Jesse James, who was right there holding my hand every time I had to "push," so to speak. Aware that I was trying to meet a publishing deadline while preparing to relocate to another state, Jesse's emotionally supportive, empathic nature proved invaluable. Jesse also enhanced the poem's aesthetics, edited the chapter introductions, and fine-tuned their poetic tone, with delicate phraseology adjustments. Jesse also wrote our final chapter introduction on the new moon.

I bow to the beautiful energy and dedicated efforts of each of these six aforementioned women, who co-created this manuscript with me, over a very intensive and laborious, yet also exhilarating and exciting, last month before publication.

Thank you to Camellia Stadts, the wonderful spark that started this third anthology, for her enthusiastic and persistent urging that we start another book project.

I extend my gratitude to the three very talented artists whose work beautified our book in magical ways. Lisbeth Cheever-Gessaman, of *She Who Is Art*, created the gorgeous artwork adorning our front cover. Our main interior-illustration artist, Shailie Dubois, offered lovely moon sketches to usher readers into each chapter. Tammy T. Stone digitally painted three illustrations signaling our three book sections.

Many, many heartfelt appreciations, to our amazing publisher, Alice Maldonado Gallardo, of Golden Dragonfly Press, whose mixture of professionalism with warmth, and efficiency with good humor, never failed to lift my spirits during production. She is a true gem!

Lastly, I am profoundly grateful to all the inspired and empowered, wonderful women that entrusted us with their words, their courageous hearts, and their valuable insights. It is an honor to serve your beautiful voices, and wild spirits. Your willingness to let me do so is the heartbeat of the *Journey of the Heart Poetry Project*. May such loving sisterhoods continue to decorate our planet, as catalysts of creativity for the awakening woman!

PART I

Awakening

Chapter One

New Moon

“The Witches believe we are all parts of a whole:
like the phases of the moon.
Together, we complete the circle and bring balance.”

Amber Argyle

NEW MOON

BY JULIA W. PRENTICE

Same as the new moon, our stories can be invisible and hidden, not seen or even thought of yet. Astrologers see new moon energies as holding all possibilities at once. Within them lay opportunities for fresh starts, new beginnings. So we too begin a journey, one of writing poetry and unwinding the wonder that is ourselves.

Our seeds have been dormant. Now, they feel the pull of tides and warm bath of sun, nourishing the rich earth below. Creativity that may have once been buried deep, pushes its way up towards the light. As poets bud, they need nurturance: support for the blossoms that may weigh down.

Speaking our truth, while at times an exhilarating act, can also exhaust us too. As our path appears before us, our own heartbeats become louder, and we turn our vision outward, gazing at ourselves as we tread.

At this time, we often begin search for our tribe, connecting to our sisters in word. Urgency rises to chant with others in the darkening night. Sometimes the way is not clear, but we are drawn to the circle.

Around the fire, listening and telling tales of wonder, builds us up and awakens us to new power. And as we wander into our words, underneath her rays, the moon will guide us: her silvering beams, as slim fingers, pointing us toward her next phase and our next phrase.

"Writing poems has been deeply healing for me. When I feel isolated from others and, ultimately, myself, I turn to this sacred act of writing in order to deepen my connection to the universe. This has made me feel less alone, or has allowed me to dwell more mindfully in the space of aloneness to see what's going on there. I can't imagine my life without writing poetry!"

TAMMY T. STONE

NEW MOON

BY RUTH CALDER MURPHY

There's a new-born moon
—whisper thin—
in the midnight sky.
The night is clear as epiphanies,
celestial bodies brilliant-bright—
and here am I,
in barefoot communion with Mother Earth,
witness to another birth,
drenched in darkness,
silver-laced,
Autumn kissing my upturned face,
my soul a sponge for stardust
and Serendipity,
absorbing magic and miracles
in a moment
of infinity.

"Poetry is a lens through which I examine myself to learn more about the me I was, and the me I am, and the me I might become! Writing a poem, for me, is very akin to a birth process to bring a poem to paper...and I believe birth is spiritually initiated. No creation exists without creator, and whatever that creator is lives inside me and causes words to spill out."

JULIA W. PRENTICE

MY FIRE SPEAKS

BY JULIA W. PRENTICE

My fire speaks from anvil bones,
Its language forged
With hammer and tongs.

　　Forged in my heart
　　Smithed in my soul;
　　My fire erupts.

Gouts of flame spew from crucible lips,
Sparks fly from my nostrils.
I imagine them destroying everything.

　　Almost dragon,
　　I breathe and speak conflagration
　　Words landing on the page
　　White hot burning,
　　Or only smoldering,
　　Their smoke can tempt with
　　Curling tendril fingers.
　　Beckoning the unwary
　　To my flame
　　That leads to annihilation
　　Or to redemption.

Not knowing which ones
The fire will temper
Or destroy utterly,
I bandage up my fire
Smother the blaze
Until no smoke is left.

Only ashes remaining
And so protecting
All those vulnerable ones
From my burning words
        I snuff myself out.

MUSIC IN THE WORDS

BY VRINDA AGUILERA

A writer is continuously playing with the push and pull tension between immersion in the flow of creative expression, and lamenting the absence of it when it somehow seems inaccessible and beyond reach. I have found it helpful to navigate these lapses of words by relaxing into the resistance, and seeing where it will take me. The answer is very often a surprise. The muse can be a fickle friend but I have a secret: she loves a good game and will often come out to play! What are your '*what ifs*'? Use the prompt '*what if*' and write a poem of your own, melt into the 'what ifs' and see what comes up for you. Hint: be playful!

What if I can't hear the music in the words or the words in the music?

What if I can't keep time to the beating rhythms of my heart,

Or see the vermillion red color of my blood pulsing like a freight train through my veins?

What if I can't feel the deep, existential yearnings of my soul,

Or locate the bruised place inside where I keep that shadowy, dark hole?

What if I can't see the blank, white spaces where I should paint with a pause,

Stroke with a comma or decorate with a friendly clause?

What if I can't taste the subtle sweetness of a sunrise on the morning morrow,

The tattered and salty tear stained edges of sorrow?

What if I can't detect the honey lavender noted memories embedded in a scent?

Or measure the length of a thousand meadows of regrets past and spent?

Dance to the rhythms of the music in the words, close your eyes and sway to the lyrical beats

The words in the music soon will follow, overflowing from your heart's inner soul seat.

WRITING MYSELF FREE: THE STORY OF AN ACCIDENTAL POET

BY TRACIE NICHOLS

I was eleven when I wrote my first heart-cracked-open-wide poem. On the surface, writing it was an assignment from my art teacher. Looking back, I think it was the Universe priming my poetic pumps.

We were asked to write a poem in response to an art film depicting stampeding horses. The film was a torrent of close-up images of wild eyes, mud spraying, masses of jostling backs, heads and colts falling behind, all to a relentless soundtrack of hooves hitting turf and frightened and excited squeals, neighs, and grunts. It was visceral. Powerful. Dangerous. I remember my heart thundering nearly as loudly as their hooves, breath caught as if I'd been running with them.

Our assignment was to watch the film, then immediately write what we thought and felt. I sat frozen and confused while my classmates busily scribbled. Then, suddenly, words pounded out from somewhere deep in my core into my hand with the same torrential rhythm of the hoof-beats I'd just witnessed. I had no idea what was happening but, like the colts, I was swept along as the words wrote themselves in my notebook. Afterwards I wasn't sure if I was excited, ecstatic, or terrified. All of them, I think. I just knew I wanted to do it again. Even though I didn't have the words to describe my experience, some part of me knew I'd touched a resonating strand of the sacred. Since then it feels like every poem I write weaves me more closely into communion with Oneness.

Writing now...

Now, when I write poems, it's full body/soul adventure. The process starts when I see, hear, or imagine something that sparks my curiosity, or when life happens with unusual intensity and I'm exploring my inner terrain. The seedling poem will tingle or hum in my marrow and muscles, as well as at the back of my mind. The tingle percolates around and through my belly, finally ending up swelling my heart until words blossom out my mouth or hands.

For example, one morning I spotted a few crow feathers standing upright in the grass and that spiraled me into wondering....

Who were you
when you
flew?

Why did you
leave them
behind?

While the pain of a turbulent childhood etches itself into...

There are screams
inside.
They're trapped
in my bones.
Secured by sinew
so they don't
sidle out.

There are so
many holes

some of my bones
whistle, now.

I'm a bone-flute woman.
I moan when the wind blows.

That's what happens when things are working well. Sometimes, though, poems get stuck. Then I have what feels like verbal heartburn. It's irritating and uncomfortable and I feel....unfinished. It drives me to whimsically wonder if my bone marrow makes poems along with new blood cells and if some future x-ray might reveal stray, stuck stanzas.

Public or Private?

When poetry rises from deep, wounded places I'm not always certain it's meant to be published. I do think there are some poems I will never share. That said, when it feels like sharing the poem will help expand someone's worldview, or help someone feel like they are seen, heard, or not alone, I usually take a deep breath and publish. It's certainly true, though, that poems, like *Bone Flute Woman*, (excerpt above), that reveal I'm feeling flayed and infinitely vulnerable, can be hard to share publicly.

Poems help me blaze trails through terrain that both explains and expands the essence of who I am. I use poetry to help me navigate, and to help make sense of the ebbs and flows of a constantly changing life. Staying curious, looking with eyes and a heart willing to be awed, this is what helps me find a poem in everything from a simple feather to complex relationships.

I firmly believe all people have poetry flowing through them. Whether it comes out as words, or in colors, yarn, fabric,

HTML or other code, theoretical math, cuisine, inventions, or something else, releasing the poetry humming in our bones helps us explain ourselves to ourselves, and helps us introduce ourselves to the world.

Life flows tidally. It seems we're always navigating incoming or outgoing waves of change. My poetry weaves a sturdy boat for me to ride those waves with my curiosity and confidence as sails, often shouting "huzzah!" into the wind.

Where does your poetry take you?

TRUTH

BY MARIANN MARTLAND

there is a longing within. it sits somewhere between desire and pain.
it dances with me,
twisting and twirling around the loops of my veins.
it knows how to pull me into deep despair and then leads me to blackened paradise.
it grows, quickly, like a seedling reaching for the light,
touching with hesitance, knowing the fire scolds and scars.
it grasps at desperation with the intensity of infatuation and lust,
but holds steady with the commitment a new born brings to living.
swiftly, it transforms into melodies of belonging.
sitting with ease, yet creeping through blood and bone.
no release is granted as it makes a home inside the ache, becoming comfort.
it lies dormant, quiet, alone,
until life and death reignite its insistence to be seen, to be heard.
it scratches through skin and taps on the windows of my eyes,
calling, screaming to be realized,
demanding a moment to be known, to be felt,
to be held.
there is a longing within. it sits somewhere between desire and pain.
and it is held.

"Since I write most of my poems when I'm processing difficult emotions, the biggest lesson I've learnt is that any emotion, however strong and overpowering in that moment, will pass. For me this is very comforting, and I remind myself of this fact when I'm battling whatever freak-out is happening inside. Going through older poems, I can reread some of my struggles and I know that shortly after that whatever I was struggling with passed. Or at least the intensity of it passes and by writing through it I shed light in my dark corners. From this practice I better understand myself and how to weather the storms in my mind, making the writing of poetry most definitely a very cathartic, spiritual process in my experience."

Jenn Grosso

MY VOICE

BY CATHERINE GHOSH

She hopes to exit unnoticed
tiptoe out the back door
swirl into the canopy of trees
and dangle quietly with the Spanish moss.

She slips through slivers of opportunity
out through the open window
across the pastures and hay bales
to the soft sound of the Mourning Doves.

But I hear her
scratching at the periphery
of being and becoming:
the rusty writer who doesn't write,
hiding under the autumn leaves
as I rake them into the bonfire.

I hear her screaming in the flames
as I take pen to paper
and the crackling inferno at my core
extinguishes any wilted remnants
of the mute within me,
at last!

because

by Isabel Abbott

because the dreams of the quarries returned (the unknown of what rests beneath, welcome and wanted, right after crashing into cold water, how it would almost feel like flying more than falling on the way down.) and so too did the late summer peaches.

because a man once walked an unauthorized high wire between the twin towers in new york city on an august morning. to "discard…and reinvent my art."

because the ankle strap on my orange vintage shoe broke that night, and when i asked if she had a safety pin, she said,"here, what size do you wear? you can wear mine."

because in ancient egyptian, celtic and hindu cultures, the owl was guardian of the underworld and protector of the dead, a seer of souls. and sometimes knowledge is doubled edged: sharp and dark and liberating.

come out, come out, wherever you are. because in the end, eros was burned by the light. and this was his strange salvation.

because when i was seventeen, i sat in high school english class and wrote out the poems we studied onto my skin, pale flesh of thigh and arm up to elbow, with a ballpoint pen. and somehow this is why i trust.

because my bed makes sense to me now.

because our lady of guadalupe, the dark virgin, is the patroness of the mexican armies during the wars of independence. and also is the mother of maguey. and wears the colors of the toltec divine couple ometecuhtli and omecihuatl. because she comes from loss and finds a way to speak anyway. because she is willing to be used, to be what is needed, in order to find a way through.

because i am not superstitious. except, i am.

because there was a plant cutting, in a glass jar, sitting there in the shower among soap. and it was beautiful, a thing so hopeful and regenerative. and how else do you explain it except to say this was the moment when i knew.

because when jacob wrestled with the angel, the wounding was the blessing. and the ladder goes in both directions.

because when i stood outside in the night, looking up at the moon with him, this boy that came from my body and is forever his own, i knew he was the purest and most complicated love i will ever know.

because some people speak of a calling as clouds clearing, a great voice from the other side of the woods, and a path made clear like seas parted or cornfields after the crop has been harvested and now you can see again to the place where ground meets sky. and i do not have or know this. or if it happens, i have yet to recognize my own name. still, i'm walking in.

because in the dream, she told me the name of trees. and i wondered if they were scarred or marked as chosen, when names were carved into wood, and if they knew or cared or made such a distinction, or if this was only mine.

because timing is everything.

because in those stories, she opens and she eats and she sees.

because, when we had coffee that last time, before he moved back to Iran, he told me, "you are perhaps mistaken. you are not a rebel, going against the rules given you. you may be an outlaw here. but it's more. it is so much more. you are simply your own country."

because she survived her past to arrive in the present. and you can call it whatever you want. survivalism. luck. relentless hard work. whatever name given, i will take back the year that the locusts have eaten. sit out on the back steps in the last cling of heat, her mouth like honey and wine.

because my love is for reality, what is here, and only ever here, once.and this is poetry.

because of all of this, these things, i want to say that yes, maybe it is true, i have what i once assumed foreign or unfit for my temperament and terrible stories. a kind of fidelity or conviction in the movement towards light, even as we walk on the dark ground we will return to. a stillness in the unanswerable questions. a choice to create a geography of meaning.

faith.

NIGHT'S LAMPPOST

BY SUSIE CLEVENGER

Hung from night's lamppost January's winter moon
drops starlight bread crumbs along my path
to guide my feet to her tabernacle
where spirit and flesh commune with the sea.

Standing in siren footprints I feel her song
lift daylight worries from my breast.
I am united with renewal; purged by
the tide washing away my unrest.

Change nurses each cell in my body
strengthening my resolve to lift
praise for years of life, to be one with joy,
to reflect an open heart with my countenance.

Freedom is bookmarked with lunar light.
I've become a pen rewriting dreams,
an editor removing doubt from a manuscript
only I have the power to write.

"I write because I believe in words. I write because I do not believe in words. I write because it is a dance with paradox. I write because you can play on the page like a child left alone in sand. I write because it belongs to the force of the moon: high tide, low tide. I write because it is the way I take long walks. I write as a bow to wilderness. I write because I believe it can create a path in darkness."

Terry Tempest Williams

THE BODY TRANSCRIBED

BY ALISE VERSELLA

The feather quill can scratch out beautiful words. But first it must draw blood. You must bleed the lyrics of your heart song. They must mix with the salty brine raining from the valleys of your eyes, to form an intoxicating potion: A carefully balanced alchemy.

Portions measured out and weighed against hypocrisy. Shed the blankets of your winter flesh and anoint yourself anew with the sweat from the brow of your lover.

Offer the naked heart beating in your throat. Offer your voice.

Shout out the song of your soul and stamp out the soot of your past life.

The ashes of the fire warm the new skin covering the vulnerable, newborn bits with pulsing red and blue. And like the leather over a drum the organ beats like native thunder, burning like a star, scorching a blaze of its truths across the skies. And rain: Rain from the darkest depths of your soul—scratched out from your hollows—will flood your rechristened pages.

Chapter Two

Waxing Crescent Moon

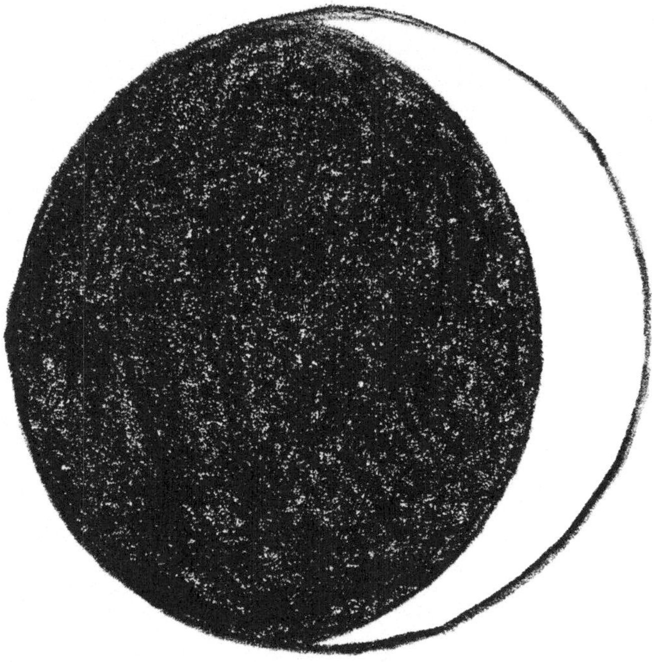

"Just like moons and suns,
With certainty of tides,
Just like hopes springing high,
Still I'll rise."

Maya Angelou

THE WAXING CRESCENT MOON

BY SHAILIE DUBOIS

Wrapped in a blanket of twinkling stars, she rests peacefully. Witnessing, her dreams frolic with excitement. Soon, they will be awakened by the light of the Sun—drawn out of the land of dreams, set on a curious path of becoming.

The Sun's golden rays embrace her like the touch of a returning lover. Filling her with a warmth that cannot be contained, overflowing into a childlike laughter. We see her radiant smile hanging effortlessly in the night sky. She is the Waxing Crescent Moon. Sharing with us her wisdom: that darkness is a rich and fertile soil, nurturing us in our dreams.

The Waxing Crescent Moon marks the beginning of a new creative adventure. What emerges from the darkness and moves into the light is a manifestation of our focus and intentions. When fear overrides trust, we desperately cling to our own ideas and draw from a limited pool of resources. Our restlessness demands things to happen now to cope with the feeling of being out of control.

Coming into the light with our hearts aligned with Spirit, an inner sense of direction and purpose flows throughout us. We are shown the next step that takes us deeper into our souls: learning how to be of service to others, and to contribute to the enlightenment of humanity. When we say yes to divine inspiration, drawing from an infinite pool of resources, we are spiritually supported in bringing our dreams to life. Just like the Sun brings the moon into her fullness.

The moon shows us the divinity in our ability to create. She pulls us into a creative flow that is free from worry or fear, teaching us how to be in a fruitful relationship with the divine that is rooted in love and trust.

In exchange for our open and willing hearts, we are offered the spiritual gift of creativity. Poetry, like all art forms, is not forced or contrived. Rather, it moves through us by divine inspiration. When we acknowledge the spiritual source of creativity, there is no end to the beautiful things that can emerge from our imagination. In opening, we create a wonderfully magical place where we can commune and play with Spirit.

Imagine our dreams like a seedling blossoming into a flower. To reach its full potential, the seedling moves towards the light. In return, it is given everything it needs to blossom. The Waxing Crescent Moon holds the same wisdom, which can be seen throughout the natural world. What if we lived this way? How would our creative endeavors change, if only we stepped down and let Spirit lead the way?

The Waxing Crescent Moon activates our memory of who we are: beings created so brilliantly that we draw to us—as if by magic—everything we need to become full radiant beings. All that is required to move into our fullness, is knowing faith and trust.

POEMS OF YOUTH

BY TAMMY T. STONE

In the mid-nineties, I moved to Jerusalem for my third year of university. I was a journalism student coming from Canada; I had to squeeze a busy four-year program into three so that I could study in the Middle East and explore life in a country so entwined with my ancestry. It was soul expanding and heart opening on many levels I'm so grateful for.

In addition to courses in the Hebrew language and Middle Eastern politics, I gravitated to a creative writing class taught by a truly inspired teacher; near the beginning of the semester, she encouraged us to keep a journal exclusively for writing down our childhood memories. It was a revelation. What was there to write about? In so many ways, I still felt like a child, though by then I already had a continuous stream of journals, many in three-ring binders of grey and maroon my dad cast off to me from his work, in which I'd been confiding my innermost thoughts and feelings.

At first, I stared at the empty pages, unable to remember much at all, certainly nothing concrete; this surprised me to such an extent that I'm still profoundly shaken and grappling with what it means to confront the gaps in our own narratives, what the absences mean, or tell us about ourselves.

The memories soon appeared, haltingly at first, and then in ripe, full, if still siphoned off pieces. I was starting to become acquainted with myself in a new way, as a picture unfolded of a little girl I didn't know as well as I thought I did. I was learning that the past is not a fixed entity forever dwelling in a contained space, but something both fickle and malleable, even changeable in the face of our contemplation. I started to understand that I have a part to play in discovering and molding the ongoing story of me.

Eventually, this exercise triggered a memory from a previous trip to Israel a few years earlier, when I was on a youth group tour. One day, we visited Yad Vashem, Jerusalem's much-visited Holocaust memorial museum. In a sea of unspeakable sadness, particularly haunting is the Children's Memorial, a space designed by renowned architect Moshe Safdie, carved out from an underground cavern; the first, striking impression comes from its arresting darkness, and then, the tiny candles that flicker throughout the subterranean, hollowed out space. On a very long loop filled with pregnant pauses, a recording calls out the names and ages of the approximately 1.5 million Jewish children who died in the war.

I was just broken by the time I emerged into the glaring sunlight. I could not process or at all comprehend what I had just experienced, the magnitude of the loss and suffering, the relationship to my own family history, that I'd had the privilege of being born and raised in such different circumstances; I stumbled somewhere away from the crowd and cried and cried. A little later, our group leader told us about a famous poem written in a concentration camp in 1942 by a little boy, Pavel Friedman, two years before he was transported to another camp, where he was killed two years later. Our group leader turned to me with his soft, brown eyes. "Would you read it for us?" I wasn't sure I could get through the poem and my impulse was to hide and be alone with the swell of feelings inside me. But I also intuited the momentousness of this occasion, how precious it was that a group of newly-connected young people on the cusp of adulthood – yet still so close to the children we'd been – were leaning on each other in our shared history and tender, maybe even ancient, grief.

I read the poem, called "The Butterfly." It was my first time reading poetry aloud to a group of people, and as I read the beautifully-wrought verses, hands shaking on the piece of paper (I can remember it was a black-and-white illustrated photocopy) I could feel deep in my heart the way words serve to unite people across the boundaries of space and time, and hold us in sacred acts of discovery and regeneration; the way words can breathe from one soul to the next, giving voice to the Truth of experience when we falter in disbelief and incomprehension at life's harder realities. I felt the dawn of a realization I'd have again in a few year's time, writing down my childhood memories: our words can heal us.

I didn't realize this until now, but I think that this memory has never truly left my side, like a little childhood wish placed under my pillow; I think that in many ways, with each poem I write, I'm trying to come close to that powerful moment of awakening, expression and communion gifted to me all those years ago.

THE GREATNESS OF NOTHINGNESS

BY ZAHRA AKBARZADEH

Carving inner emptiness at midnight:
"Come here and gift me your light!"

Sweeping the dust off the way:
Looking, singing, waiting all day.

Pouring the ocean in one droplet
you and I drink of this couplet.

Singing beyond an ecstatic song
bubbling mind has faded so long

Thrilling a whispered "ah" in my ear:
Splendor of the dreams, "O, my dear!"

Who shakes the rhythm of the dance?
Who makes the rhyme of the voice?

No name, no shape, no shade of color
No eye, no ear, no pain of labor

No mind landing to fly high
No word saying but a deep sigh

Silence; the sentence of happiness
Secret: the greatness of nothingness.

THE INVITATION

BY PEGGY TABOR MILLIN

Writing—a hall of mirrors,
myriad reflections of myself
holding blank pages.
No exit, no partner but fear—
until I listen:
the quiet hum of my heart
the beckoning whisper of my soul—
an invitation to attend,
RSVP engraved in script
and in my hand
a golden pen.

I accept and lose myself
In the dance.

THE WRITER

BY GINNY BRANNAN

How do you describe someone
with depth of thought.
emotions etched inside her words
and heart worn on their sleeve?

We hang on the snapshots of her life...
the love, the anger, the hope.
the dreams, the joys and sorrows...

We follow her down sunny paths
and decaying streets
and see life through eyes
both jaded and hopeful...

For her story is our own,
we recognize ourselves in it—
and we are touched
changed forever in the reading.

DIVINITY

BY DOLLY MAHTANI

My dear child,
Why are you restless?
Why are you hurting?
What are you searching for?
Where are you looking?
Sweetest child,
You have been lost for so long
but I see you now.
Let me show you
the road that will guide you home.
Remember, sweetest child,
remember who you are.
Truly, Deeply, Infinitely
Who are you?
You are...
The majestic sun that rises beyond the horizon
You are...
The spring that has just arrived.
The hero of your own life.
The warrior. The kindness agent. The dream maker.
The philosopher. The gardener. The healer.
The photographer. The artist. The musician.
The nomad. The label-breaker. The treasure.
The diamond. The student. The guest.
The star. The instrument. The butterfly.
The feather. The cloud. The bluest sky.
The rock. The scientist. The lotus.
The dragon. The swan. The passenger.
The key. The pearl. The projector.
You are the blank page. You are the entire damn Saga.

You are a soul. You are Concentrated Energy. Know this.
Know the light that you hold. The power within.
Know your worth. Discover you're limitless. Admire yourself.
We are everything we have ever searched for—
We are love,
We are peace,
We are happiness,
We are truth,
We are beauty,
We are bliss.
Know this.
Feel this.
Be this.
Allow yourself to shine through all the fears around you, and just...
Be.
Dear child, I beg of you
Remember your divinity.

MULTIFACETED AWAKENING

BY AMANDA DOBBY

Today, I awaken. It is a beautiful, crisp, cold and windy January morning; the full goddess moon has yet to surrender the sky to the rising sun. I can hear the call of alluring sounds and that of a crow perched in a tree outside my window. As I open my eyes to meet the new dawning light of day, I notice three figures standing in my dimly lit bedroom.

At first I am afraid, but as my eyes begin to adjust, so too does my heart and mind.

The first is a young girl, maybe about 9. Her hair is brown, curly and frizzy; huge, thick and wild, hair like medusa - or maybe like the branches and leaves of a willow tree in full bloom. It is short and ends in a harsh line at her ears. She looks very sullen, very quiet and withdrawn, very serious and sincere; there is no smile near. Her gaze cuts right through your soul. In her hands she holds a book, which she clings to as though it is her only prized possession; she is holding the weight of the world in her heart, and salvation in her hands.

The second is slightly taller, slightly older, but no less serious and no less sincere; her eyes are deep pools and mirrors of fear, still penetrating and mysterious because in truth she is no less than a seer, a growing goddess who knows only who she is not, and not a trace of who she is. Her hair is pulled back in a tight bun. If she wears it down, the whole world seems to stop, and so she keeps it hidden instead of showing it off. She is wearing baggy jeans, an oversized sweater and running shoes. She appears to be about 14, but if you ask her, she will say that she feels much older. She is a child who has chosen to take the weight of the world on—and her tiny mind cannot not comprehend at this time how her frail body will eventually come to suffer; she is being used as a family distraction and buffer.

The third is a beautiful woman who is looking worn and tired—in her eyes there is no more fire, no more mysterious desires working to conspire. She has her hair tied back in a messy bun and wears no makeup; jeans and a sweater clothe her petite and muscular frame. She has a baby balanced on her left hip, and a small hand is interlaced with hers to the right. She holds both the hand of the sweet child, and the body and weight of the precious baby. She's known cancer, loneliness, abandonment, loss, disappointment and grief; she has also known birth, nurturing, love, growth and life. She is only 27, but her years of self-punishment, self-sacrifice and self-neglect have left her much older on the inside.

Slowly, I rise from my bed and take a few steps forward to kneel at eye level with the young child figure.

"Good morning, my innocent inner child; I see that you are hurting and that you are unhappy today. I want to tell you that I see you. I know the other kids pick on you and that you feel different. I know that you feel like no matter what you do, you cannot make your family happy and that all you want is to see them smile. Why don't we go and fix that? Shall we dance and play and put a smile back on your lovely little face? That's the best way to make people smile."

A wide grin breaks her thin lips, and she begins to nod wildly, causing her short hair to bounce and shake. I then shift and shuffle my position to kneel before the second young woman. I want to look up at her, not at eye level or looking down.

"Good morning my dear, my beautiful mirror. I see you—I really wanted to tell you that. I see that you are hurting, and

I see that you look unhappy. I know that they still make fun of you. I know they laugh and snicker and call you fat and ugly. I know they told you that you are messed up and crazy. I know they told you that your brokenness was the source of all their problems. I know you keep trying to fix what isn't broken and you're breaking your magnificent self even more. Do you want to know what I have in store?"

A slight, sly smile starts to break through her solemn frown.

"We are going to draw and paint and read and explore the forest pools and floor. We can dance like no one's watching and sing like no one cares; we can drop our feet into the cool clear waters; there is no need for us to hide from the world's harsh stares."

Her sly smile became a megawatt grin.

I then moved myself in front of the mother. I greeted her small shadows with silent and simple kisses planted on their precious heads, for I would soon greet them again. I looked up into her sullen and serious eyes.

"Good Morning Great Mother Moon Goddess who is trying to hide. I wanted to tell you that I see your beauty, your uniqueness, your strength, your courage, your drive and your powerful inner vibe. I know that you try and try and cry and cry and that you often ask yourself why—why and what did I do so wrong; and how – how can I do better and more than I have done before; how can just I alone restore. Do you now want to know what I have in store?"

She was too afraid to move, might she unsettle the children, too fearful of upsetting the tenuous balance.

"We are going to play and sing and dance with the others like the innocent children that we are. We are going to enjoy this amazing life that we have been gifted. We are going to read a thought-provoking book; we are going to do some coloring and we are going to draw ourselves a hot bath and light some candles like the passionate self-lovers that we are. We will go to bed early in sheets that are fresh and clean and we will wander through the forest that will come to be home someday in our dreams."

"Come on my loves, let's go—let's go begin our new day."

The figures connected hands and melded to become one, and just before this was done they melded with my own sinew and flesh, and this I did not detest.

I smiled. I gave thanks.

I walked out and into the bedroom of my oldest, my son. Three smiling figures were standing in his room: a young boy; a young man, and a man, and all were smiling fiercely, so I nodded to them joyfully in turn— then I woke my young boy with a song and dance.

Together, we then went into the bedroom of my youngest, my daughter—I silently nodded and greeted her bright and smiling figures too - and then we woke her with our song and dance and to this she replied by also jumping in to dance, and we dressed and brushed our teeth in a joyful trance.

We made chocolate chip pancakes for breakfast.

To my son, as he walked out the door to catch the bus for school, I said, "I see you, I know you and I love every bit of you and whoever you will come to be."

To my daughter, as I hugged her goodbye at daycare, I said, "I see you, I know you, and I love every bit of you and whoever you will come to be."

And so begins the day for a family who knows they are made of asteroids, history, fresh futures, pains, triumphs, love, letdowns, energy, moon dust and stars.

Don't forget to love every part of you and who you have been; know that you belong amongst the stars and just knowing this will help you to see yourself and heal your scars—this will take you and those you love very far.

A FLOWER IS LIKE A CHILD

BY MELISSA E. MARTINDALE

(Edited by Julia W. Prentice)

a flower is like a child
it starts out as a seed
you feed a seed with water
sunlight and fertilizer
you feed a baby
with mother's milk
nutritious food and vitamins
that seed begins to develop
first, the stem grows
(hopefully the stem will be sturdy
given warm sun, gentle rain, rich soil)
a baby begins to develop too
the baby grows into a child
with sturdy limbs, strong body
(hopefully the people around her give her love,
strong virtues, morals, understanding and encouragement)
the flower becomes a swelling bud
ready to spread its petals wide
if the child has been given all that she needs
she will be able to handle all situations
if the flower is well nurtured
the blossom will be bright and vivid
the child, well cared for, is now an adult
grown, changed, now bright and vivid
she spreads her brilliant petals
just like wings, and flies

PO*ET*TREE

BY ALISE VERSELLA

It
Began with
A Wrinkle in Time
I was twelve and exploring
A world after the sturdiest of apple trees were
Reduced to splinters in a rotted apple of a city, trying once
Again to find its roots, trying once again to bear its fruit. I was
Growing and expanding in my twelve year old mind the way worlds were
Expanding for Meg Murray, tesseracts in parallel universes, trying to find my roots
So I dug my roots into poetry and found its leaves in the scenes of movies, like in The Color of
Friendship when Congressman Dellums gives his speech. It brought tears to my eyes and that's when I
First learned what words could do. How they can stir the birds and bats flapping in the maturing heart
Fighting for nesting space in a foreign tree. And A Ring of Endless Light illumined how those same words
Could soothe all the broken wings. The Notebook was more than just a sweeping romance for it
Introduced me to Leaves of Grass, and I was swept away by a man long since buried in "This Compost".
A man whose branches covered me in his shade of wisdom. It was the wisdom of rhyme that helped me
Comprise my own. When speech failed me and I was terrified, felt too shy; unfit, not popular just weird
Rhymes took my tangled sentences; knots in my stomach and made sense of the mess of my
Adolescence. Because I found poetry in everything: The roaring seas, the trees
Po*et*tree; my sapling green now sturdy. Words are fluttering birds in the knotty nests of my hair
Poetry is in the air I breathe when I reach out my branch limbs
It's even in
The rhythm of
My heartbeats.

Chapter Three

FIRST QUARTER MOON

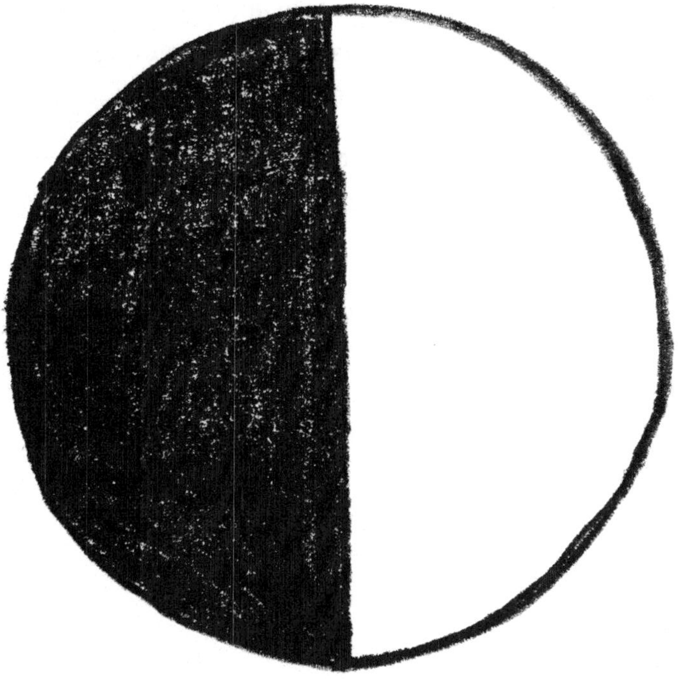

“Now is a time when the wombs of women are telling sacred stories that give life to the deadened spirit, walking the streets, plugged in, on the go. *Do not lose heart*. Not now. All that is true in you is magnified: accelerated in the moonlight.”

Alison Nappi

FIRST QUARTER MOON

BY ANITA GRACE BROWN

The moon, or Luna, bemoans: "My gravitational pull, no matter how powerful, will never moisten my dry landscape with the Earth's blue seas. *I want to be you*: with your endless generative creation and evolution." The entire galaxy seems to be shouting: "YOU have not done enough, not *been* enough!" Meditating on the relationship between the sun and the moon, I imagine what it must feel like when you know you need masculine energy to illumine your beauty. Surrendering to this kind of humility requires a girl to embrace her sacred woundedness.

How many women worry they are nothing but pitted rock on the inside, possibly beguiling from afar, and relying on a man to complete them in their worthiness? The first quarter moon, being half shadow, must embody a solid sense of alchemical transforming of dark into light.

This chapter's works represent our human transit through self-discovery in its early stages, which can be fraught with this kind of anxiety. Our lovely Luna has forgotten her betrothal to the sun before the dawn of time. Our celestial sister and brother are ONE!! The moon's own denigration diminishes a part of God. She has no need to hide a part of herself and yet her very nature is to obscure pieces of herself from our eyes. Does she wonder if the 'real me' is safe to reveal only on occasion?

"When we are unkind to ourselves, energy is drawn away from enlightenment, and into the ida, or moon channel." Sharon Gannon. It is then that we, too, question if our shadow self is safe to disclose. And yet a deep respect for mystery and interconnectedness overshadows this initial concern. Writing creates a path through the rocky terrain of our inner landscape, guiding us to the truth about ourselves.

When we first begin to flex our writing muscles we might feel similarly. We might often compare our work with others we admire and end up feeling inadequate. Trusting our voice as one of a kind, and very much needed in the world, is difficult early on in our journey of self-expression. Though we may share our words, we have yet to discover our connection to universal concepts and consciousness: our place in the cosmos.

Because we all know—there is nothing new under the sun!! Why write? Why continue to expose our deepest, darkest secrets in hopes of making the subconscious, conscious? Most of us find we have no choice: writing becomes an urge, a practice as close to us as our life-blood, of integrating life experiences through putting them into words, and sentences. Often, this writing becomes the way we connect to the Divine inside.

Contemplating our moon's potential for low self-esteem, she mirrors back our own inner battle with our shadow. Even Shakespeare, in Romeo & Juliet, wrote: "Arise, fair sun, and kill the envious moon, who is already sick and pale with grief," as Juliet compared herself to the sun with its fiery display on the horizon each morn. It seems natural our lovely rock moon, in her simplicity—no roots, seeds or doves—would gaze at the big blue marble as if her celestial Mother were the perfect female specimen of fertility. As we mature, we discover the flipside of envy is inspiration.

In astrology the moon defines the unconscious state of our character. In other words, it signifies an area beyond our consciousness. This unconscious state has always existed and it will always exist as the all-pervading power that encompasses the entire universe. The Moon also represents productivity, femininity and developed feelings of motherhood within us.

With her reliance on the sun for illumination, our dear moon must, on her darkest days tell herself a story of being disconnected from her source of life. Does she trust that all is spinning, moving and changing moment by moment: nothing staying the same for long? On her own she appears to produce nothing; yet, her true nature represents all the unmanifest energy—the raw material of everything yet to be created.

Our days are brightened by sun when our moon forgets her power. By night her 'lesser' light governs our sky. During first quarter moon (also referred to as half moon) her emergence is exciting!! Writing with hearts and minds as one demands authenticity and requires vulnerability. There is such a fresh, youthful vibration behind the poems in this chapter. And yet, Human nature resists being hurt as our very bodies tense anticipating being re-traumatized.

The energy of this moon is one of expansion toward full illumination but we imagine she personifies our own longing for wholeness. The truth is: *we alone have always been whole!* Fully human and fully divine, we travel in spirals of remembering and forgetting, and remembering again.

Howling our desires for unity, we spin into ecstatic aliveness as writers when the world expresses appreciation for our offering. Glimpses of our oneness of being with all of nature, God and Spirit give us encouragement to continue voicing our truth. Contemplating our moon—united with her sun—makes the entire earth spin around on its axis. Yet she forgets this so easily and returns to bemoaning her worst qualities. The writing life of a poet often mimics the same cycles.

I FOUND MY SPIRITUAL AWAKENING IN POETRY

BY ALISE VERSELLA

My spirituality lies in a different kind of verse
You cannot find it in the numbered psalms at Sunday morning church
It lies in wild stanzas, fluttering sparrows, bleeding ink on a blue veined perch...

I have never been a very religious person. Although I am Catholic, I have never found spirituality in the walls of their churches, their songs never made me want to exalt in praise, and I found no comfort in the tissue paper pages of their bibles.

History class had taught me of the wars fought over a god, the blood spilled in his name. There seems to be a hierarchy in being a "good" Christian, as opposed to just being a good person, and spiteful eyes are always looking down at those who sin differently than they do.

No, I am not very religious, but I have found spirituality in that open expanse of wild nature; it calls out to the wildness inside of me. The soothing salt of the sea, the verdant green and smell of pine, the warmth and cleansing sweat of golden, pulsating sun, the gentle lullaby sung by that man in the moon while I lay awake writing under his light.

And how quickly it can call to arms its forces and ravish me. The roiling sea can wreck the ship of me, the earth can quake beneath my feet and set to fire the roots of my trees, the sun can burn through a false visage and the moon can bleed red into my howling lungs.

There is also the kind of spirituality from songs found in records' dusty grains, hidden tightly in a milk crate. Songs that have made me sing out through my tears: "Gimme, gimme shelter, oh before I fade away;" I've found my saviors in Lennon and the Lizard King, felt pure ecstasy in the voice of Janis and Mr. Fogarty. And I have exalted at the first few chords of that song they say had pleased the lord, Hallelujah.

I have found those same saviors in the fiction books that held my prayers more closely than any bible, Torah, or Koran. I have written my bleeding heart into their margins, my lonely tears often blurred the ink poked words. Those stories hold more of my faith than any sermon delivered could ever preach. Because while both proclaim demons exist, only those stories say it is I who has the power to defeat them.

Haven't we all once felt like that heavenly host? Like that rebel angel cast out for wanting too much? Wasn't Eve always hungry for more than just an apple? I am starved for something Catholicism cannot give me. I am only satiated when I am writing.

I found my spiritual awakening in poetry.

I have found my camerado in the open road with Whitman, found salvation in Eliot's Wasteland. I saw the light "burn, burn, burn[ing] like fabulous yellow roman candles exploding like spiders across the stars" in Big Sur with Kerouac. My soul howled alongside Ginsberg and his "hipsters burning for the ancient heavenly connection to the starry dynamo in the machinery of night." It is in poetry I have found my connection to this world, this vast yet contradictorily small world.

I have found the power of my own voice. Seen my dreams turned reality in the push of ink into paper flesh.

I have learned to further understand my flesh. The subway lines stitched across my palms; how my lungs cushion a crevice deep and dark, protect the fragile heart locked in its curio cabinet of rib bones woven together like the wicker of a basket.

There is something of the confessional in professing my sins in metaphor and simile proclaiming it in stanzas, setting it free. Within the slant of my lettering I find myself, embrace my darkness and free myself. The waters of poetry baptize me anew and in those waters I am cleansed. My spirit freed from its crown of thorns, inside a poem I am blessed.

My spirituality lies in wild stanzas, fluttering sparrows, bleeding ink on a blue veined perch and I rise and I fly on long forgotten wings and I soar between the tolling of the bells in the towers of your church and my heart converges with the stars in my eyes and what emerges from my soul is holy.

DREAMS AND OTHER FAIRY TALES

BY CAMELLIA STADTS

Sinking deep
as the moon makes its descent from the sky.
I'm falling into dreams
that have me sharing my night
with the stars.
I reach for a comet that flies overhead,
but remains nowhere close,
except in my dreams.
My dreams surround me
with colors of coral and turquoise,
as I realize that I have fallen to the ocean depths,
trusting that these dreams not let me drown.
I slowly rise to the surface of my journey to the underworld:
It leaves me wet and wondering
as I float to the top of consciousness.
How did I manage to fall so easily?

AND I WILL AWAKE

BY CHERYL ANNE BRATMAN

I remember the day
You sang me awake:
Came to take
all heaviness away.
I remember the play
of light amongst the branches,
the opening of my eyes,
swelling of my heart;
the spritely spring in my step.
I remember the color:
the deep blush of pink
that dared me to think
beyond the "facts"
as they had been presented.
And Your Sweet Beauty
has not since relented,
though You have at times
gone into hiding, having found
me too long confiding
in dryness of paper,
and cold of stone.
But You have never
left me truly alone,
and will not let me
fall back asleep...
at least not for long.
For the rain of Your Song
will tickle my roof, and call
me out from where I am hidden.
The warmth of Your golden gaze,

unbidden, will once again clear
the haze from my tired eyes,
and lead me toward the great surprise
of the light and color of my own happy heart.
The refreshing rain
of my own song
will kiss my face,
and I will awake.

MYSTIC POETRY DWELLS WITHIN THE SILENCE OF THE DESERT

BY JENNIFER HILLMAN

I look for inspiration for my poetry, or perhaps it is more like the inspiration comes to the poet who is open to receiving the beauty within the moment. As I write most often in the early morning while still in a meditative state, I trust the wisdom graced upon me and simply write the words from the experience of the innate connections. Through a vision or a deep feeling, the words come and I write those inspirations down in a poem.

I've lived in an actual desert for over 25 years, learning to understand the beauty within this arid, lucid land. The wisdom of survival is available in every part of the desert. Finding the simplicity of living life fully, while being still, empowers the mind to let go and trust the natural order of life and its eternal grace. This empowers me to express the beauty within the magic found in this place through my poetry.

The mind's journey through the desert comes within the physicality of life. To me, the mind dwells in dreams within the dream. Surrounded by the arid land of wonder, convincing one to continue on and on...in search for something, what? Only the mind knows, yet looks outside at the dry, hot and seemingly empty space of dust. Yet this seemingly empty space is the land where I met the Goddess Isis. Sometimes, for the mystic poet, the mind needs to appear empty first, like the desert, before poems reveal themselves. As the vision of Goddess Isis did to me on that day in pure white light: powerful, yet feminine in grace. Then she spoke:

"Look, Child... look around you and see... each grain of sand is you; you and all your aspects, lives and adventures. The dreams you have lived, the dreams you have died for, the love that lives and dwells within you... you are a survivor. Each grain has a message for you. A beautiful love note of solitude and grace awaits you. Sit within with the mind and absorb your truths within each grain of sand. Remember all of who you are now. The sands of time never forget and always forgive."

Isis faded away and I sat down in the warm sand, feeling the grains between my fingers knowing all is revealed to those who are patient and focused with intention.

The mystic poet within me gives rise and shines in the sands of the desert. Many eons of dreams, and poems are born within these dunes. Each one brings promise and heart, delivering my soul to life... and to death. When a poem is revealed to me, I become the child of the stars, who has come like a dewdrop of morning sunshine upon this land:

"Dream now ... breathe in the truth that lives, like the raindrops of the cloudy skies ... the tears of your heart ... like the blood inside of you runs, pulsate through each moment. Come with me into the depth of this place called your heart. The center, like the sun, gives life to all your dreams. Your truths that dwell in this space, a life in waiting. So you learn of patience and persistence in this place. This is the space of intuitive guidance, where you gain the open door to the wisdom hidden in your soul. And give it voice in your poems."

How I come to realize the well of all that is hidden in my voice does not generally come to mind immediately. Trial and error serves its purpose. The different ways, and pace, of walking across the sands; the time of travel; the distance, and the convenient methods of giving up and surrendering help me express my voice. Surrendering to what? To the desert, to the elements, to God, Source or Truth; or simply to self and the God-spark that dwells within. All of this longs to emerge in my poems! The voice of the Goddess resounded within me, reminding of this:

"The soul has memory banks; with the help of your heart, it brings all your wishes into the physicality of the mind and into manifestation. Trusting yourself, is trusting your heart, your soul and the Universe that lives within. There is nothing more you need to trust. You are all you need for your dreams to come true. And with this trusting wisdom, the secrets of the universe are yours for the creating. So, go now. Live to the fullest this moment allows, and know it is all in perfect order, as you created it to be so."

"As Above, So Below. In the splendor of the ages, you bring forth all that is around you. Understanding this brings all the sweetness the world has to offer. Enjoy this moment as the sands of time are collecting them to be remembered and forgiven with grace unto midnight's full moons each month.

"Time is as endless as you are. Speak your truth with kindness and the universe will be returning the kindness. Your motivations are changing like the shifting winds across the sand dunes, surrounding you with much magic to serve you and serve you well as you understand the secrets revealed to you now. Trust, dear Child ... trust yourself and smile."

Then the Goddess Isis faded into the moon's brilliance, leaving me with a deep, blissful feeling of love, and a valuable message: That the mingling of my mind, heart and soul brings the magic of my poetry alive with each breath: breaths that are breathed in love and kindness, exhaling beyond each moment in time and into eternity.

Looking at the vast openness of the desert, I felt the immense peace of my own spirit writing poems upon the pages of eternity. My writing practice trusts in such magic! I feel it and see within every time I look at the stars in the desert night skies, or center myself in the mystic's journey. The journey within my mind is my ultimate poetic practice, as I dance with the magic of the unlimited beauty whispered in those moments. And when I return from such moments, I always give thanks. For they remind me, that for the mystic poet, there are always wells to drink from, even in the driest of desert landscapes.

I AM

BY TAMMY T. STONE

The words come in strong
A wintery defiance
I am
I am this
The wind, in its blustery scattering of Truth,
Won't relent
I am a writer
And now it is said

I am a writer because
Words come unbidden
Fill the space around me
Chimera glazed with sun
Living embodiments of half-remembered
Dreams of other realms,
Of my time before this

A writer because my hands open wide
Making an innocent of me
As I hurl myself into their curves
Spilled from mountain caves
And the underside of leaves
Because my eye is trying
With every breath
To anchor in the heart
So that the words I see
Will find their way Home

The bamboo rustles from the
Core of the Earth

Until every last Being
Hears the Call
Be what you are
I will always catch you

MOONLIT

BY MARGARET BEDNAR

She resides like a goddess,
alabaster smooth
beneath moonlit branches,

alone, untouchable,
even morning's mist
hesitates to come close,

but within her perfectly
sculpted breasts, she longs
for a loving touch, satin sheets

and a reason to blush.

LET THE MOON'S NECTAR TRICKLE OVER ME

BY CAROLYN RIKER

I write on a similar path as the moon caresses the sky. She shows herself to me. My emotions and thoughts tempered as much by her shadows as her light. I hold with deep respect the changes of my femininity. Age is also playing a role as I see myself step into her truth and find her voice. It is through these temperate transitions of tenacious insights, I write.

The moon is at half and I feel her growing energies within. I learn from the split of dark and light. Peace comes from facing and untangling our shadows. I watch the moon as natures candle light; it glows an inordinate amount of wisdom. I listen and feel and learn to follow her guidance. She has mastered the tides of the sea and has much to teach me.

There's always something magically when I look to the sky and know, we all share a stellar cloak of the heavens. This poem sprung from a restless night when the half-moon's presence comforted me.

The moon, in her half fullness
resting on the edges of nothingness
the seen and the silence of quivering darkness;
she speaks to me.

She teases the tendrils of thoughts spilling
and words tangled in the depth of distant starlight;

the intensity of energy quickens by day
and by night, I feel her graceful beams reach
a soft space of ebony and clarity of insight.

The flipside of the moon,
the half hidden shadows, lit by dreams we remember
and memories we can't forget;
she captivates our inner glow
and awakens our candidness.

I am the moon and she is me
we dance a rhythmic melody of ebb and flow;
our mysterious femininity unfolds
and age becomes our gifts
as lush as a ripened mango.

The moon,
in half her fullness echoes the
waves of the sea
the song of storm and tranquility;
tonight, let me tip a moon slice into my cup
and let her nectar trickle over me.

FREE-WRITING: A WRITING EXERCISE

BY TAMMY T. STONE

Free-writing is a beautiful writing practice that can help delve deep into the subconscious, and discover what is stirring within. And it's incredibly simple to begin! All you have to do is sit down with a pen and paper —you might even use a special journal for just this purpose— and choose a time you will write for; 15 minutes works well at the beginning. Then, get poised to start, and write without stopping. No stopping to think, refine or edit; just see what flows out of you! You can always start by using a prompt, for example:

I am most scared of...
One thing I've always wanted to do is...
I'm so thankful for...
If I could overcome one challenge, it would be...

Or, you can just begin. You might feel you have nothing to write at first, and you may feel your writing is boring, and this might be frustrating. Hang in there! The key is to remember that this writing is just for you. No one else ever has to see it, and it does not have to be "good," or elegant, or live up to any expectations you might have for your writing. The important point here is to have fun and to not stop writing during the time you've set to engage with this practice. Bad grammar and run-on sentences? Go for it! Don't try to edit yourself; just be free! By continuing with a flow of writing, you are able to short-circuit your rational mind and take yourself places you might not have known were in there, ready to bubble to the surface, for your observation and contemplation. Who knows—you might find a goldmine for future poems or prose in there… Enjoy!

For this piece of free-writing, I gave myself the intention of reflecting on the moon as I sat down for a free-writing session:

ABOUT THE MOON

What if it's true what they say, that the wisdom in the moon is the wisdom in me? What if the wise ones know this to be true, but I can't understand this in my heart, where it matters? I've spent a lifetime acquiring knowledge and taking pride in this and valorizing the quest to be learned and to have knowledge like it's a possession I can eternally hold and value, and all the while, I didn't have the awareness that there is a gap between this way of being in the world, and a whole other way, a magical unheard of realm and that this way was readily available to me anytime. Anytime! I've seen it in fairy tales and walked in its midst during family trips to places for hikes and canoeing, and even during much smaller excursions to the front lawn, that first grassy frontier, with my sister, where we'd climb up the crabapple trees, up we went, not under the moonlight, maybe, that time of day was for sneaking into neighbors' spaces through the backyard bushes, what a giant and labyrinthine adventure that always felt like!, but under the bright suns of our childhood. I can even remember what I wore one of those afternoons, maybe many of them, a shorts and halter top set made of thin cotton. The top was sleeveless button down with a collar and you could tie the bottom of it into a knot, and the whole thing was printed in a geometric design of deep jungle and tigers. I remember how brave I felt in that outfit, how wild and of the earth, how my green eyes shone with a power I don't know if I've ever experienced since, and in these activities, the wisdom I've spent so much time seeking recently existed in full bloom, uninhibited, in its pristine natural state, though I'd never yet gazed up at the mountains, and maybe didn't know how to penetrate the hearts of those I loved, which is to say, the wisdom of love was buried so deep in my own heart and what a lifetime of work, wresting it from there. Yet, when I look at that little girl now, wearing the jungle with the tigers, I want to caress her soft cheek and eager-to-please eyes-heart and tell her, yes, go there, the jungle has everything you want to discover. You can come out once in awhile, and be nice to your little sister, but carry the wild jungle in you, and when night comes, look up and be bathed in the shimmering moon wisdom pouring down over you. Let this be your movement and your legacy and your wisdom, sweet girl.

SISTER

BY GRACE GABRIELLA PUSKAS

Poetry is one of the most powerful forms of expression. Both our thoughts and words are vibrations, affecting both our internal world and external environment. We have great power to create and heal (or destroy) through the language and intention of our words.

All life can be equated with sound, with music. We are living in a uni-verse after all! In this sense, medicine-poetry is a great healer and can act as Blueprints, or energetic upgrades, actively changing the cells of our body and our consciousness.

This poem was expressed in alignment with the very energetic-ally powerful Solar Equinox and New Moon in Virgo in September 2015, and first shared as healing Medicine Poetry just after a soul sister's Reiki Master sacred attunement ceremony. It has only ever been shared once, and in a very sacred ceremony, therefore I share it with you now in the hope that you feel free to share through guided meditation, sacred ceremony or medicine circles, for the unifying of our hearts and higher selves and for true collective consciousness sisterhood. This healing poem takes us on a journey through time and space, to the roots of our cells. I truly hope it resonates.

Sister, you are a healer: a channel for the divine!
You spell secrets through your thoughts, that subtlety
    seduce my mind.
Your heartbeat pulses pure vibrations through the air,
    through the ether,

My auric field receiving these angelic messages that are
intended as my teacher.
My sister, do people know of your magic?
Do others feel the mystical essence of your thoughts:
telepathic?
Can they see your aura glow and shine,
Or hear you truly, deeply, from your cosmic rhyme?

Your words are spirit travelling through the unknown,
Each specific with intention, rich with substance, yet in
flow.
You are Music, the Source in its essence:
An ancient memory expressed through pure innocence.
Each sound I feel and each moment satisfies
My soul, my heart, my mind; I sense your inner goddess
flies!
Your golden wings fully spread and free...
It is through ancient eyes we see.

Eternal sister, a true shamaness you are,
Sounds synchronisticaly swimming through both our
mouths:
Both these Stars.
Our souls fully in charge and steering our paths,
The wolves by our side, walking gracefully in our hearts.

Crystalline temples appear wherever you glide,
Long lost secrets of Atlantis slipping through your smile.
Water droplets of memory glistening in your eyes
as you whisper secrets of wisdom and love, vibrating out to
raise our Light.
Dearest sister, we have been here before!
Here with Gaia; many lives,
many more.

Why do you return my love? Do people feel your pain?
Do they see your selfless choice of returning to this game?
Infinite levels to master and complete,
Always choosing to dream the light back into Gaia
grounding it through human feet.

A true shamaness—a conduit for spiraling galaxies,
Medicating through meditation to tune in to your galactic
family.
I see you sister,
I see your soul through eyes gaze,
Your mind lingering through the spaces, only memory
remains.
Your ancient heart's drum taking us in a journey; a journey
through time and space,
Through many realms, worlds and dimensions, travelling
freely with love and grace.

Without your bravery, love and devotion,
How would we hear of this magical potion?
How would we experience an Angelic Goddess in human
form?
Would this world ever hear the call?

Earth is speaking to us: we feel her words.
The animals singing for us vibrate in tune with her verse.
This uni-verse we perceive with all its different notes
Divinely reminds us to slow down, breathe,
and tune in to the groove's tone,
the heartbeat, the flow:
That primal pulse that is innocent and free,
not separate from him, her, you or me,
connected to sun, sea, bird and tree.
WE are the notes:

The healing melodies here as remedies for Gaia's growth.
Our crystalline vessels signaling us to change its cells,
Our diamond matrix in a new timeline; a new heaven,
No more hell.

These wings have been hidden for thousands of years,
The eye of One, all seeing and knowing, as clear as the
seer's.
Illusion's veil that hid is from our dreams,
Kept us lost in the maze whilst our powers were deceived.
Sister, I can feel your third eye:
I can feel your emotions like the ocean's waves
And hear your mind's madness like our loving sun's rays.
The eternity of your being radiates to my soul,
Your in-finite infinity secure, safe,
at home.

So please my love, brighten the world with your light!
Inspire hearts through your song... you truly are beauty
divine.

PART II

Blossoming

Chapter Four

WAXING GIBBOUS MOON

"I am not the same,
having seen the moon shine
on the other side of the world."

Mary Anne Radmacher

THE WAXING GIBBOUS MOON

BY NANCY CARLSON

"For nothing is secret, that shall not be made manifest: neither anything hid, that shall not be known and come abroad."
Luke 8:17

This waxing gibbous moon can be called the "moon of endings," as it is preparing to reach fullness, to be complete. Like love, it feels anticipation, a pause, as if "birthing" and almost ready to push something wonderful out. Like the movement of spring, buds are breaking through the earth. Seeds have been planted and have been growing to reach this place of readiness to manifest. Yet they are not fully developed, nor illuminated.

It is an exciting time; a feeling of blossoming and energy is increasing within us, rising to a crescendo. Growing in appearance and intensity we move toward fullness. With fertility and creativity there is the promise of a flower, a love or lover, new beginnings, fruition and perfection. Like spring waxing into summer, there comes lightness and brightness.

A feeling of zest for birthing a poem, or prose arises, releasing and letting the words spill onto a page, as nature assists. Our words and ideas are cultivated in the moon environment. Refining, editing and finishing touches are being done. We begin to release and let it all flow out of our hearts, bodies, minds, and from a higher source.

What consumes us at this time is growth, learning, creativity, healing and positive transformations, all arriving in divine order and timing. We feel ourselves trusting that what is coming into form is perfect, as it is.

As poets and writers, we are reflecting, seeing the bigger picture, and knowing that no stone is left unturned. We are curious of what will be, allowing our instincts and intuition to direct us. Despite traveling the "mountains and valleys" of our heart, we continue to go forward and arrive at our destination, fully manifested. This is the inspiration Mother Earth provides, with the glorious influence of her waxing gibbous moon!

Our words are outpouring into the world with a desire to interact with others. The moods of this moon can illicit perseverance despite obstacles that do not serve us, and barriers we need to cross. Through poetry and writing, our expression of words can bring deeper levels of fulfillment, awareness, consciousness and compassion. We deliver that to others, and ourselves, by creating harmonious caring and a flow of hope. With that, our uncertainties lessen and confidence increases.

Nature continuously provides these lunar cycles for our own development. Over and over we have the opportunity to assess, reflect, feel, learn and grow. As we move toward the fullness of each lunar cycle, we have a chance to do it again, and again! This lunar phase brings excitement, accomplishment, curiosity, organization, growth and meaning in life. We have time to adjust, refine or change our minds.

In becoming more aware of the moon's phases—how they affect us and how often they change—we no longer need to search for meaning. That knowing is in all of us; we just have to tap in, and pull it out through the writing of poems. In doing so, we give words to the knowing that is always within, and in all of nature. This wisdom is free: a gift from life to us. One of the ways in which we unwrap this gift is in the writing of a poem. In doing so we find meaning, as we all walk our path together.

"I hope you will go out and let stories, that is life, happen to you, and that you will work with these stories from your life--not someone else's life--water them with your blood and tears and your laughter till they bloom, till you yourself burst into bloom. That is the work. The only work."

Clarissa Pinkola Estes

WAITING

BY TAMMY T. STONE

I sit dreaming in a city
brimming with our most
colorful fantasies
watching people go by
swimming with the
words within

Waiting

Waiting feels good
on a bright day
like today
when it all comes to now.

It is now that lives.

"No more writing myself out
Love, Beloved,"
I hear myself say
in the blinding light
that washes everything away.

So I fill the day with love,
painting it deep in
my heart.

Later, the moon appears
misty and dim
in the warm blanket of night.
She glazes the world whole

and under her resplendent,
soft eye,

I arrive, for just a moment
at Wisdom,

where I wash
in purity's glow,
and smile

and love
some more.

PREPARED TO SING

by Cheryl Anne Bratman

I am yet steeped in night
winter-dark and cold,
but You, O Morning Sun
are rising in my soul.
I feel You moving now:
Fluid full and free,
fiery sap of Spirit
stirring once again in me
love sweet unrepressed
no shadows to be found
deep woundedness redressed
as You warm dry bones and ground
O Bright Morning Sun
flow forth Your coming Spring;
My feet are poised to dance
my heart prepared to sing!

"Writing poetry touches a part of me that is quite deep, and that makes me happy. At first I was a little embarrassed by my poetry, but through the support of other women, I began to slowly share it, as writing poetry offers us a chance to play, to be ourselves, to experiment, and to speak to others in ways that we usually don't on a daily basis. Poetry is a stilling, and a calming, a quieting that allows me to hear more clearly what is being spoken to me in my heart, opening me up to different perspectives. It's enlightening! I am so grateful that poetry has brought me this gift!"

PRANADA COMTOIS

A SONG IN MY HEART

BY SHERNAZ WADIA

Resurrect my song; tease it out of its confines
Bait it with the lure of love, to alight
Like a gentle lover's kiss, petal-soft
On the wizardly notes you waft.
From their mingling, let there be no parting.
Song and singer, melody and music maker
Must glow as one. The loved and the lover
As a sacred flame must burn

So let the sorcery of your flute begin.

SINGING FLUTES & POETICS OF LONGING

BY AMBIKA TALWAR

wild sage
wanders between rocks
singing flutes

Poetry appears like this sometimes. We walk into IT unaware that we would meet a poem. And IT would meet or find us. This IT (a poem) is simply a moment when something magically and instantaneously comes alive in us and transforms us.

Such a thing happens more often than we realize. It is as though we suddenly become aware of our innate capacities connecting with all that is vibrant and enlivening outside us. So our inner and outer worlds wink at each other as we move through life.

The instant the inner and outer cohere, a whole thought is birthed—indeed, it is already present as seed. Each moment we encounter awaits its manifestation in form. Whether it becomes a poem or an insight is not the point. The point is we are, in essence, continually creative beings and we create continuously. We are poets even if we do not write poetry.

singular flute
singing beauty of stars
rainfall of light

We each are a "singular flute" awakening to our desire for exploration, an *autopoiesis* through which we recognize each singular expression and destiny as a unique voice. Also majestic are fragments of various singular destinies. Thus, in a world wrought by dire conflict and confusion, we recognize in this rain of light, that we collectively are carriers of virtue. But we must change our actions.

If what we are about to create has not yet become apparent to the conscious mind, it is already creating itself. When we actually become aware of this sudden winking, we are delighted, surprised, and enlivened. We feel we have an unusual privilege to explore and express our deepest longing so we may cherish life and be nourished by it.

Thusly, we are each a poem inspired by our own reflections. In turn, may we inspire each other.

sparkling leaf
our eyes prisms of joy
dancer's carpet...

Inspiring each other, we sparkle. We enter new worlds, which we create. Such prisms of joy surround us that every particle of us is entranced by beauty in our midst. Indeed, this weave of prismatic joy is a dance. We are continually in motion; our creating is a dance.

Imagine, if you will, moments of great insight, of excitement and wonder. Imagine being transported into other worlds where sparkling crystals mirror our delight. In such a state, let our witness self note how we move, halt, lift a hand or finger, pause, smile, weep. Note how our friend sings, runs, winks. Note how our child beseeches our indulgence. Note how we arrive at every step aware and enlivened. Perhaps, we are distracted by this delight and may be in a state of forgetting! But we know.

Our inner ear listens to rhythms in our patterns, how silence marks our step. Every act is a dance of delight, wonder, eros, courage, disgust, anger, victory, disgust, comedy, sorrow, laughter and tears. Such aesthetics weave the carpet we stand and walk on.

We are weaving a new carpet because it is time to do so. Shall it be woven with beauty and intelligence? Will shadows give it dimension so it continually awakens? Or will shadows pull us into obsessions that lead us away from truth? May this weave be a foundation of virtues, so our poetry keep us ethical and in passionate longing.

rewoven gold
silk fabric endures
millennia of love

We recognize that love is an organizing principle of wholeness, a dance both emptying and filling. This *autopoietic* weaving is a unique coming to wholeness, a unitive process, and a perfecting design. It can be evolutionary for, in each moment, we have the power to choose the form and expression of our next thought and creation.

Let us remember that we are guardians responsible for the wellbeing and wholeness of all our relationships, with nature and with each other. An exploration of a new poetics is a natural result of our longing, awareness, and our essence, making poetry a "bridge to new worlds."

The poetic is our conscience residing in expanding consciousness. As we create, we endow our selves and one another with responsibility, a choiceless participation with all that is. What we choose and how we respond is "respons-ability." Coupled with desire, we create a foundation upon which we may now carve our individual and collective destiny: to become that Love we long for.

Cells love it
when we smile
even if worlds break

Nothing matters
but the Great Empty
from which all comes...

Chalice is passages
for flow of fountain

Always traveler longs
for this Void, this nourishment
flowers grow here...

Are flowers not grace? Are we not channels for wonder of divinity? Is not our body-being an ever-renewing poem?

It is this ever-renewing connection with divinity that urges our unfolding into sacred awareness. With each experience of recognizing our body-being as a chalice, we aware and arise in radiance and develop resonant frequencies for our life path despite the sometimes thorny roads we traverse.

So it unfolds as we continue the process of self-creation; living is a deeply profound practice of seeding joy and equanimity.

The time now is ripe for another re-creation of gathering our strengths, our playful wisdom, our longing, and our creativity to re-form into a new model of sentient beings, kosmic and local, beyond sustainability. Let us shed the ache of longing and face our-selves in each other's hearts. Let us gaze. So what we long for is not so far away any more.

The more me I become,
the more I see you.
I do not know yet what that means,
or looks like—
Perhaps as sky and gaia inter-are,
so are we.

I'd love for you to show it to me.
For in knowing me,
you know yourself–
as trees do
and parrots that sing in them.

Eagles tear away piece of blue
scour vast rolling green
where we walk,
as summer wind
lifts skin of puddles
and we laugh.

(Note: This current version of the essays is quite a bit re-edited and re-titled for this edition. An early version was previously titled "Celebrating Our Creative Spirit" and was published in *Radiance Magazine*, in Irvine, California.)

THE BIRTH OF A POEM

BY SANDRA ALLAGAPEN

And so it begins:
A whisper in the silence...
Like a caress in my heart
raindrops of light
falling onto my soul,
feelings turning into words
tiptoeing into my awareness,
gently at first.
Murmurs to be heard
morphing into a ball filled with colors
bouncing in my mind:
Energy seeking expression
demanding to be
acknowledged and written,
heard and sung,
seen and painted.
Thoughts as old as our existence
running through my blood
with a cry of joy
bursting onto paper,
becoming a part of me!
The silence then returns:
this time filled with stillness,
permeated with gratitude
for my presence
and willingness to give a voice
to a living world
with so much to say.
In this silence
I surrender all resistance
and vow to always listen.

MOON POETRY CEREMONIES

BY LORE RAYMOND

Like the ancient, magnetic pull of the moon, so the poetry of Maureen Kwiat Meshenberg drew me in. Four years ago, her poems suddenly appeared on my Facebook page, *Women as Visionaries.* As I found her poems affecting, I asked myself: "Who is this woman whose words touched my core? Her words quickly became a daily part of my spiritual readings. I cherished them, and began to integrate them into my daily, spiritual rituals.

Over time, my friendship with this beautiful and inspired poet deepened, and for three years Maureen contributed as the Visionary Poet to my other Facebook page, *Women as Visionaries with Lore Raymond Magazine.* It gave me great pleasure to share her poems and watch them affect other readers. Especially, as the poetry began to reflect the waxing and waning phases of the moon! For it became my habit to share the dates of the new and full moons on the magazine's editorial calendar. It was amazing for me to see how the moon theme drew in other writing sisters, who also embraced the moon dates with their inspiring posts.

In my openness to integrate reading poetry as a daily practice, from 5 to 15 minutes a day, I found that as the moon was increasing or decreasing in her light, so was I, all supported through poetry—the soul's language of light. Suddenly, I felt at one with the moon's phases unlike ever before! This connection began to manifest in the form of Moon Poetry Ceremonies that reflected the timeless feelings in the ebbs and flows of my life, and the lives around me.

Surrounded by other women, I sought to honor the Divine Feminine within us, and in all of Nature! We created moon altars or shrines in special places: our bedrooms, the beach, favorite garden corners. Upon these altars we placed special items to help guide our meditations: a silver tray, a silver or crystal goblet, purified water, indigo colored candles, lavender oil, incense. At the center of our altars always rested a printed copy of the prayer poems we'd be engaging: for each phase of the moon, the energy in each poem shifted, as did the energy within us.

As these Moon Poetry Ceremonies began transforming me, I found that their transformative power was affected by how I approached them. To make sure I was in a receptive state while participating in the rituals, I asked myself these questions: "Are you coming to this time feeling rushed, judged, or judgmental? Tired? Or are you full of enthusiasm, excitement, and expectancy!" De-cluttering my inner and outer self prior to the start of each ceremony tilled the soil for planting the seeds of moon-given realizations in my heart.

Today, I give thanks to the moon, to the inspiring sister poets who revived my dialogue with the moon, and to the online forum that brought us together! Each day, as I continue absorbing and breathing in this magical and mysterious energy of the moon, I marvel to think that it all began with a poem! We women can have such an uplifting effect on one another, if only we remain open to it: ready to receive all the gifts that life places before us. I invite you, dear reader, to open yours.

HERE

BY JAMIE BURGESS

Here is discomfort and vulnerability:
skin stripped bare—heart, bones and blood lay exposed.
Here is jagged air and raspy lungs—
an urgency, a restlessness, an itching desire to pull away...
to run far and fast until I hit the comfort and cover of the
    shadows.

Here is knowing, and moaning, and a time of rebirth:
full of revelation and acceptance and courage.

Here is fullness of breath, and softening of heart.

Here is deciding to stay: to create a home in the light—
planting both feet into the earth, and sprouting deep, tangly
    roots.
Trusting. Opening.

Here is the magic that comes from holy water
and sacred ground
and the beauty of letting go.

WORDS I HAD FORGOTTEN

BY AYALA ZARFJIAN

I traced words on leaves,
with my fingers and my toes.
I scattered them in the orange grove,
and watched how they were swept into the heavens.
The fields nearby were peridot green,
inviting and unassuming.
I knelt down,
wishing the scars would heal,
and I could find them once again.
The sun shone with regret,
attempting to console my emptiness.
The wounds of life led me to abandon
the words I love as I buried them deep inside.
Poetry, my old friend,
you found me while I played hide and seek
with my words.
While I wrote them on napkins and receipts
and tossed them away.
Poetry you found me in the ocean,
on a moonlit night,
the tide was rising,
the fish were biting.
You found me and I could no longer hide.
I had forgotten how you heal me,
how you awaken my desire,
how you let my soul dance outside my body.

"It is easiest for me to write poems about my connection to the Source. When my heart is wide open, I find that the words, like life, just flow through me—and not from me—as if the poems have their own unique voice, wanting to be born. My poems mainly emerge after walking in nature, dancing or meditation, but also from periods of longing, deep listening, and reciting a mantra. I feel myself to be an instrument of the poems, facilitating their births, not the creator."

Savitri Talahatu

A HOLY YES

BY CHERYL ANNE BRATMAN

It seems I began composing little poems as soon as I could write. My grandmother kept a poem I wrote for her when I was six years old, and I remember writing a poem for my first grade teacher to accompany my homework every day for the entire school year. Even before I began school, I loved nursery rhymes, the cleverness and musicality of the words.

My teen years were spent writing dark, angst-ridden poems that filled notebook upon notebook. Poetry as an outlet for difficult circumstances and feelings likely saved my life at tumultuous points along the way. During this time, I also began writing song. The songs became my priority as I began singing professionally, and music became the primary channel for my creativity. Then I experienced an intense spiritual awakening and the poetic floodgates opened, and have not since closed.

For me, the act of poetry is an act of Love; it is nothing short of Divine Intimacy. I am wooed by Beauty, Depth and Wonder, and must respond by exploring and extolling the Sacred Source dwelling in the space where that creative impulse burns and churns. Giving myself to that space and opening to its gifts is a fiat, a Holy Yes to the movement in my soul. It has come to be that most of my active prayer takes the form of written poetry or spontaneous song. I suppose it's only natural that the inherent creative impulses, which became apparent at such an early age, would be my natural means of relationship with the Divine. I am so thankful for this gift, and the ways in which it informs and enriches my life. I hope that in sharing, it somehow flows forth to bless, comfort, or inspire others as well.

THE JUMPING SALMON AT DUSK

BY SHAILIE DUBOIS

Of the tears that fell
one grew cold
It flowed down my cheek
filling the valley of my breasts
with an icy stream

The jumping salmon at dusk
they moved me

How could their splashes
awaken a tsunami
The waves crashing
in my pond like eyes
ushering a hot stream into this world?
How could the weight of their soaring bodies
Bring a pen to a piece of paper?

Yesterday, a Native man passed me
as I sat by the mouth of the river
"Have you seen them jump?"
"Yes!" I replied
He smiled, "It is amazing, isn't it!"

His words
they followed me
into my dreams
and surely into eternity

How could the salmon move me to tears?
The Salmon are free

The Salmon are unquestionably everything they were
created to be
They are exactly what God has been asking of me:

"JUMP FOR JOY!"
"SPLASH!"

MY JOURNEY TO BECOMING SHAKTI

BY DARSHANA MAHTANI

I use my poetry as a way of mixing my love for words with my love for knowledge, and aim to create poems that awaken spiritual consciousness. I love writing poems that make one think, question, discover, and rediscover. I long to share with others the knowledge I've acquired on my own journey of self-love and self-discovery. Most importantly, I want to help people connect with who they are and what they are here for, through my poems, as poetry has a natural ability for touching hearts. My wish is that my poetry may touch souls. I put a little piece of my own soul into everything I write.

Poetry is my courage; armed with ink. It keeps me open, vulnerable and kind. It makes me honest and free, sustaining my generosity, beauty and creativity. Poetry is the language I speak; it is the language I hear. It is the world that I understand and the one that I hold most dear. Therefore, I cannot talk about my poetry without speaking first about my life, my history, my heritage and the spiritual practices that are an integral part of who I am.

I come from a Sindhi family. Both my great-grandparents fled India during partition. Their homeland is now a part of Pakistan. Twenty nine years ago, a Sindhi boy from Barbados decided he was ready to get married, flew to India where he was shown a photo of a Sindhi girl from Chile and agreed to the marriage. A year later, I was born on a beautiful island in the Caribbean.

From a very young age, I was surrounded by the teachings of my Hindu culture. I dressed up as Goddess Laxmi for Diwali, the festival of lights. I played Goddess Sita in our yearly play of the ancient text the Ramayan. My family attended Sunday programs where we chanted bhajans (sacred hymns) with our whole hearts. I learned that I was a soul within a body, and that I had chosen this body to fulfill a specific purpose, and that the way to achieve my purpose was to follow Bhagavan's (or God's) four principles: Sathya (truth), Dharma (conduct), Santhi (peace) and Prema (love).

What I didn't know at the time was that I was an Empath by nature: I felt everything so very deeply. The increasing arguments between my parents during my childhood created a hole within me: a deep, dark abyss that took hold of my life. I turned to emotional eating to try and fill the void. This only worsened the situation. I was then sent to live with my grandparents in Chile in hopes that it would help. I was very far away from the girl that loved to dance and climb trees. Yet this was the birthplace of poetry for me. As many other beautiful things, it was born from complete darkness. It was a means to escape my reality: a way to express the true me hidden underneath. In this dark night of my soul, I loved playing with words and trying to make every line rhyme. They were as cheesy as you could get, but they made me so happy.

While living in the south of Chile with my mother's family, I learned new rituals. Every month, we fasted during the full moon and performed an ancient worshiping ceremony called Sri Satyanarayana Vrata Puja. For the married women, it meant praying for the health of their husbands. For unmarried girls like myself, it meant praying for a good husband. The *kathas*, or stories told during such rituals, scared me. Each chapter was more gruesome than the last one. "How could God be so cruel, unforgiving and merciless? Is this the nature of God?" I asked myself.

It was the first time I ever questioned my beliefs. However, I've found that beliefs are like that: fragile. The moment you doubt them, they crumble. Refusing to believe in a punishing God, I declared myself an atheist. As my life was filled with suffering at that time, I had to believe there was a higher purpose involved, a bigger picture, a better reason. This was when I decided to go out and find that reason for myself. Poetry was my sole companion.

The journey that followed could be summed up in one word: Love. Somewhere within me I had a memory of love. Of unconditional love, connected love, divine love. It was a love that I had never seen or felt before but I knew existed nevertheless, and that I was actively looking for it. I travelled the world and dipped my toe into different religions searching... for a feeling.

I thought I had finally found it in a person. Have you ever just met a soul and felt like the entire universe was plotting your mingling from the very start? That's what it felt like for both of us: like a supernova explosion! I wrote enough poems about her to fill a whole book. Yet, it didn't last. Fearing that human love is hardly ever unconditional, (or maybe that was just my personal limitation at the time), we went our separate ways, and I fell into that dark hole again.

Two years ago, as I was searching for something that could heal me and make me feel whole again, I walked into an unpainted house on an ordinary street in Santiago, Chile. Little did I know at the time how much this would change my life! At the door, the residing sister of the house, Tereza, greeted me. She held the door open for me as I walked in and kept her eyes locked with mine the entire time. Something about her gaze pierced my battered heart and I felt a wave of love envelop me. Gazing into my eyes with a bright smile, she said: "I am giving you Drishti: My soul is gazing into your soul." Just these few words caused a volcanic explosion in the valves of my heart. I was slowly bleeding love.

"I've had dreams about you: The Indian girl who will change the world. Welcome home."

The place I had walked into was a center belonging to the Brahma Kumaris. Today, I call it home. Some call us an organization, others a movement. We are also known as a spiritual university. In the end, labels don't matter. The Brahma Kumaris teach many things, but the one thing that I have learned from them—that has become a part of my core—is the teaching and practice of becoming *Shakti*: or a divine and empowered, feminine force!

Meditation on becoming *Shakti* involves dedicating myself to serving others, having a focus of self-study and personal growth in order to be an example. It involves being a part of a spiritual family, transforming the self, and transcending this human form, by embracing its many gifts: such as writing poetry! This practice is now my life, and this is where the inspiration for my poetry comes from.

Through writing poetry as a spiritual practice, I have learned that love and happiness are not distant ideals we need to achieve. They are our very essence! In remembering this, I no longer question my worth, my purpose, or my path, regardless of what comes my way. Once I learned to tap into the unlimited power of my being, I felt invincible! And so did my poems: now one with the unbreakable and unshakeable quality of love.

Chapter Five:

Full Moon

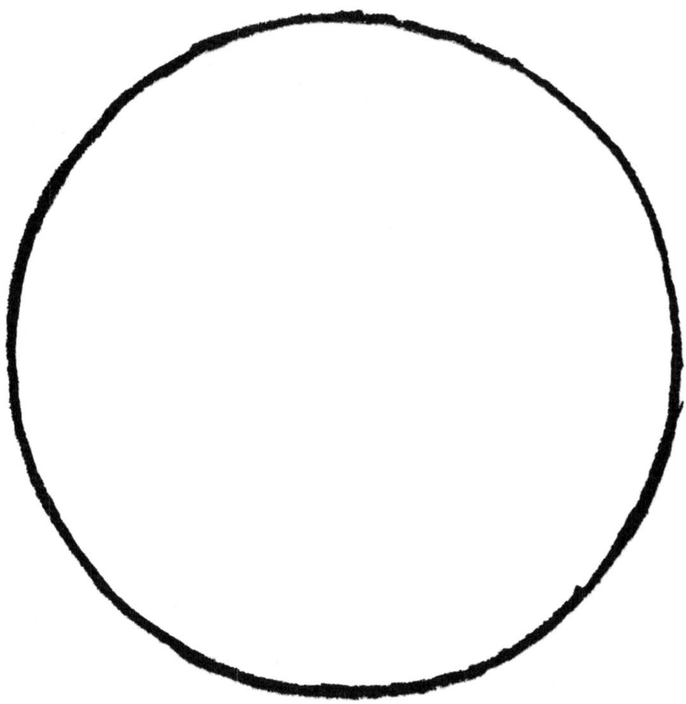

"I wake up seeking starlight
aching for the moon's glow on my skin
a child of the night
for as long as I can remember
comforted by the quiet of darkness
finding sanctuary in candles and campfire flicker
wide-eyed and hopeful in the shadows
trusting in things that can't be seen
only felt."

Jamie Burgess

FULL MOON WISDOM

BY JAMIE BURGESS

The moon has been the center of our attention for centuries. Through every culture and every time period, it has been talked about, written about, and even worshipped. Entire civilizations have revolved around its waxing and waning. Our ancestors tracked time by its movements and hunted and grew food around its cycles. Scientists have studied it endlessly, trying to grasp at its many mysteries. As much as we may try, we will never be able to fully understand its depths. All we can do, with assurance, is sit and bask in its radiant glow.

I know my own heart opens wider when the full moon lights up the sky. In its presence, I feel an intense pull on the center of my being: I become more energized, more tapped in, and more creative. I feel truly alive. The power that affects the ebbs and flows of the oceans also deeply influences me. I open up in the most beautiful ways and am able to express what's in my heart, without all the procrastination and fear that I usually get tangled up in. When I look at that big bright circle in the sky, I feel the weight of the world completely fall away. Something about its vastness and its power offers me much needed perspective.

The moon helps me to remember that I am just a tiny blip in the universal Big Picture and that my time here in this body is finite. I remember to shift my focus to what truly matters: the here and the now. And with this remembering, I immediately know—a down-to-the-center-of my-bones-knowing—that even though this body will die, I am eternal. We are all eternal. "You are made of stardust and moonlight and ocean tides," this glorious moon reminds me. And I instantly breathe lighter. I walk away feeling infinite, yet also fully grounded; ready to dig in to this one wild and precious life and truly *live it*. And that makes all the difference.

When I remember who I truly am, and what's most important, and can stay focused on these truths, I feel a sense of freedom: freedom to live fully and wholeheartedly, to love more deeply, to connect with others in meaningful ways, to shake off the fear that binds me and bare open my heart for the world to see. A huge part of that process for me is to express the truths of my heart through writing.

Poetry is the language of my heart. When I sit to write and the words begin to come, they flow out onto the page in the form of poetry. There is something so magical about the way they all come together, without any planning or pushing. They simply appear, as if my heart gently dropped them to the page, like rain falling from the heavens. Drop. Drop. Drop. The only thing poetry ever requires of me is that I open up and let go. It's really very simple, but I often make it difficult (and sometimes even painful) by getting caught up in all the details. Is it too wordy? Too emotional? Too rigid? Is it good enough? Soft enough? Poetic enough?

My creative heart, it wrestles with so many things; yet like clockwork, Mother Nature always shows up at the precise moment I need her, with these gentle little nudges to remind me: "You are perfect. All is well. Breathe. Trust. Surrender."

WHAT WORDS DO WHEN THEY SING

BY DAYA DHARA DEVI DASI

I find comfort in the silent voice,
the one that is not heard but seen.

Magic spews from the tips of my fingers,
when I'm aware of my being.

Sucked into another world,
I have finally found direction.

Being sincere with my own perception
of my past, present and future.

Healing with writing.
Healing with beauty.
Becoming more than just a creature.

Poetry has led me to myself!
Poetry has connected me to the beyond!
Because of poetry I see the greater picture.
I no longer hold on,
to that which needs to no longer linger.

Poetry is what words do when they sing.

Rhymes dance and gallop in my mind
as the pen drops a line.

Wherever I am, words flow within.

Sometimes I'm not sure what to do so I continue to move,

and before I know it, I'm sliding into more prose:
underneath the shadows I go.

Knowing that by this, I can only grow
and flourish within my soul.

When everything is in disarray,
I know to sit and wait, write a prayer,
a longing, a note, and finally
everything drifts away.

OH, POETRY!

BY VRINDA AGUILERA

Writing poetry is a mystical process for me. When I fully surrender myself unto it, I find myself immersed in a creative process that engages my entire being: my mind, body, and spirit. The mystery of this practice is that while a poem may come from me, it is also simultaneously independent of me. There is an unknown, otherworldly aspect that also lends and injects itself into this dance with words. I sometimes experience this creative energy as a mysterious personality who has many different moods and faces, who sweeps me away on adventures and transformational journeys. She, for I have given her a feminine persona, takes on the essence of whatever it is I need. Thus, she is powerful, comforting, seductive, graceful, and so much more. Oh, poetry- you capture my heart and stir my soul.

Oh, poetry, you thing of beauty.
Waiting in the shadows,
Your formless face veiled.
Humbly, patiently kneeling in servitude.
A gentle and chaste handmaiden
Cloaked and enshrouded in gauzy robes of ether

Oh, Poetry! You wicked seductress.
Shape shifting mistress of dusk, dawn
And the unclaimed spaces in between.
With your wild, untamed tresses
Your flashing glances smolder and burn.

You are insatiable, greedy
Ravaging and consuming me
With your relentless needs and demands.

You, my poetry! You're a graceful dancer.
Flowing, dipping, twirling, whirling
Mesmerizing your partner and audience alike.
Glimpses of milky white shoulders,
delicate arched neck
Your movements are hypnotic and enchanting.
Such is your magic, your spell
That each think they, alone, sway in your embrace.

Poetry! You are a swollen ocean wave,
An embodiment of nature's power.
The force and strength of 1000 barreling freight trains,
Unstoppable and indiscriminate in your destruction.
Your white, foam-flecked peaks
Like the frothy beard of a rabid dog.
At times I have been caught in your swell,
Tossed about helplessly like a rag doll.
Half drowned yet half alive.

Poetry. You are a mother to me,
I, a newborn babe cradled in your arms.
Holding me close to your ample, comforting bosom
You smell faintly of milk and roses.
Gently shush shushing,
I am lulled into a state of drowsy contentment
As we rock in a worn cushioned chair
Back and forth, back and forth,

At times, poetry, you are like a razor sharp dagger
Lethal, unsheathed and without a scabbard

If I grasp you roughly,
You pierce and slice.
Leaving your signature, an angry, red sear.
'Handle with care,' is what you tell me
If I wish to use your pointed tip as a surgeon's tool,
Lancing the toxic boils that poison and pollute my soul.

Sometimes I cannot find you, poetry.
Alone and wistful I am left wondering,
Have you forsaken me?
Then, there you are!
Peeking mischievously out from around the corners of my words
Playfully, you have been hiding
You throw your head back and laugh in mirth.
My friend. We hold hands and run off to play.

Poetry, you are my angel.
You float down on soundless wings.
I cannot look at you directly when you are like this
You are suffused with and emanate a radiant, blinding light.
You help me forget everything else
And become one with my prayers.
A divine messenger, you carry my love to my Lord.
Tunneling through passageways hidden in the innermost recesses of my heart.
Salty tears seep out of the corners of my eyes in gratitude,
I hide my face in shyness.

MENSES

BY DEJAH BEAUCHAMP

When I was fifteen, I wrote a poem about my period. I'd started menstruating the previous year, but still must have felt confused and at odds with my own body, as I was never taught anything other than that menstruation was dirty ("sanitary napkins" being the solution) and should not be talked about.

I wrote the poem in one of my notebooks, where I often scribbled my thoughts and observations, and carelessly left it lying open on my bed.

I am a red river
flowing across the earth

Later that day, my mother called me into the living room. She was holding my notebook. My heart sank into my stomach.

"*This is disgusting.*" She pointed to the last sentence of my poem, holding the open page up to my face, and I could tell that the thought of saying these words out loud was anathema to her.

My fumbling poetic attempts to understand the mechanics of my own body, to take the monthly shedding of tissue and blood and transform it into the transcendent, had gravely offended her. Did I really expect otherwise? My poetry was uncharted territory even for me, and I couldn't help her navigate the rocky terrain of my mind.

I have burst open
my body unleashed
but not broken

"I don't want you to ever write anything like that again," she said, handing the notebook back to me. "Throw it out."

I felt my cheeks get hot. I was angry: angry at her for going into my room, angry at her for reading my poetry, angry at her for trying to silence me. But I was helpless; she was my mother, after all. I had to do what she said.

I am pure
I am iron and water
I am my own mother

I went up to my room, clutching my notebook to my chest, feeling the sting of tears in my eyes, my cheeks flushed with humiliation and rage. I wanted the earth to swallow me up; I wanted a spaceship to appear and take me to another planet—anything but having to live in this house, knowing that my mom thought my writing was disgusting. That I was disgusting.

I sat on the edge of my bed for a few minutes, drying my tears, trying to process what had just happened. I looked at the words I had written, that meant so much to me. Should I tear out the page? Would she prefer if I burned it? Was I going to Hell? Were those words really so bad?

and I am pure
I have been given
the gift
of creation

No. No, I thought, something suddenly becoming steel within me. *This is mine.*

And it was in that moment that I became a writer.

Because my mother, whose opinion I both feared and respected, couldn't undo me, couldn't reduce me to her idea of what a woman should be, say, or do. I kept that poem—kept the entire notebook. Its pages have yellowed over the years, and, looking at it now, I realize that much of what I wrote in it was trite and adolescent. But it is a record of the moment when my soul knew what it was and couldn't be convinced to change course.

I spent my teenage years writing as much as I could (hiding my notebooks more carefully, of course), and as I grew older, became a wife and mother, and lived life a little more fully, I began to understand that—whatever I or others thought of it—my writing had always been *me*.

and the angels bow down
before me
and lick
the blood
from between my thighs.

As women, we are called upon to sanitize our selves, our bodies, our words. If we stray too far from earthly concerns and wander into feelings of wonder, divine connection, intuition and sexual awakening, we are called quickly back to reality by our society and culture. Often, we are unknowing participants in the restriction of the female voice. I'm sure my mother would never see her actions as restrictive; I'm sure she thought she was simply raising her daughter "right." But any time we silence another's voice we take away a piece of who they are.

This writer within me is a part of me, as much as being a mother or a daughter is. If I had decided to censor myself, to analyze every word that fell from my lips or my pen, I would have wandered through life constantly trying to play the parts most pleasing to others. Yes, I am a nurturer and bearer of children, a tender touch, a gentle word—but I am also a stormy sea, a hurricane wind, a lion's roar.

It is the same for all women. In nurturing our intuition, in letting our creativity shine forth in all its myriad ways, uncensored, we allow others to see us holistically. In finding our voice, we give voice to others. We must not fall into the comfort of silence, nor allow ourselves to be reduced to a series of labels (wife, mother, daughter, writer), but instead go forth into life as a shining full moon, whose light covers the earth.

"Don't ask what the world needs. Ask what makes you come alive, and go do it. Because what the world needs is people who have come alive."

Howard Thurman

ALIVE

BY CARRIE CIULA

Dream of gypsy travel
Catch fireflies
Spit fruit seeds
Create love
Create anything
Sip in sunsets
~Celebrate~
Take in the words of other souls...(and then let them go)
Cultivate astounding affairs with books
Dry your clothes out in the sun
Amuse yourself
Dance until you are dizzy
Revel in ridiculousness
Focus on the path that you are most attracted to (even if it is the one that is most unrealistic)
Awaken
Express who you truly are and allow others to do the same
Believe in magic
Chant "yes"
You are loved

LUNAR CHANT

BY SHANNON K. LOCKHART

oh! she appears, full and ripe, above me. every molecule of my body shakes in expectant anticipation of our dance. i feel the particles shift into the glow around me—we are one. my spirit finds the current and uncoils into the newness of the infinite.

life cycles, moon cycles, tides pulling and lifting, shaping, molding, keening and crooning me into the present, merging dreams and heightened wakefulness. bare feet ready to the ground, sensing the rhythm, the moment ripens and the meanings of my words are split open.

i am fully awake now, and flowing into the eternal, joining shyly in the poetry of here-ness. my hands feel the tug, my heart is nudged out of victim's shell, and the casing falls away into the pit of was, while the pulse of we gathers our skirts up to join in the dance of now.

i ride this surging energy into soft ferns of forgiveness, which i breathe deeply. the light shifts and the feathers of the quetzal bird are woven onto me. emerald wings shape the path, ruby fires blazing in my breast.

my feet stomp the outline of the circle that becomes my perfumed offering, whorls of palo santo and copal[1] spiraling into the journey. my senses are full, verging on too much, yet insistently pulling me deeper into the nightscape magic.

---

[1] Palo santo and copal are types of incense used in Mayan and Quechua rituals of gratitude and healing.

i am now the river crashing, running down the jungle mountain, past champas[2] and bare breasted women splashing each other while children suckle.

i am the maizal[3] filled with earthen corn ripe with the colors of ancestors, vines of frijol snaking up my stalks to complete the dance.

beyond the cloud forest, howlers screech and the current is fast. it lifts me above the volcanoes. my being throbs with energy, frenzied particles continue to peel back layers of the no-longer needed.

vestigial anger comes out in mesmerizing staccato beats, crashing into my tears, until the next wave of grateful envelops them in solidarity as they are purged. i wriggle out of the un-useful, letting it fall below into ashes.

i am running now, a jaguar alone on the mountain. i see the rocks and paths clearly in my mind's eye. i revel in the taste of discovered becoming. i trust myself to lift steps and place my feet carefully down, exactly where i need to go tonight.

the thrill of a night run in the jungle intrigues me, feeds my empowerment. i depend on ancient spirits, knowing that the moon will point out just so steps, wherever my feet falter.

i realize i want to dance naked in the moonlight.

i need my body to be anointed here...

i know that cyclical magic is happening inside me. i catch my blood and soak it back into my garden and the irises bow in

---

2 Champas are huts, usually made of bamboo or wood, found in warm climates of Central and South America.

3 A maizal is a cornfield.

gratitude at this extra kindness. i am soothed by the mundane spell of my blood penetrating the earth. we nourish each other intimately, making communal love in the moonlight as only women can. we are the life-givers, grateful gatherers, often rejected by those outside who fear the gift.

the crimson secret is ours and i embrace it each month. my ritual soothes away the trappings of an old life, fueled by fear and shame. my blood is power as my body seeks the rhythm and guidance of a universe made for connections.

the menstrual cord gently tethers me back into the earth, while freeing me to explore the voices of the comadronas,[4] ancient words that guide me through the universal. more layers are shed as my understanding sharpens. others misunderstand this dance, thinking that grace only

comes from a god-made-man who purified the offering of body and blood through death.

(the rest of the story is that he came from woman; man spilled his blood and his rebirth comes at the price of separation, and hatred.)

true sacrament flows out of our intimacies. this is the eucharist of sacred feminine flowing freely, preparing for new life in the dance of building up and letting go, back to the earth each cycle.

the mystical power of gratitude dances into the circle; it welcomes feminine wisdom birthed in splendid internal darkness, guided by the sacred light that pulls us together now, in the rhythm of this story and the glow of the moon.

i lay my pen down, and rest in the spiral dance of emergence.

[4] Comadronas are community midwives and healers. Their gifts are usually passed down through generations of wisdom collected in the indigenous groups of Central and South America.

(I often do not use capitalization in my writings and this is due to many factors. I am fluently bilingual (Spanish/English) and this style began with the Spanish rule that yo (I) is never capitalized within sentences, unless it comes at the beginning. Putting myself on par with others through pronouns makes perfect sense. I have a working knowledge of several Mayan languages as well, in which far fewer words are capitalized than in English, and over time, capitalization has become tied in my head and heart to a certain level of cultural and colonial arrogance that I wish to avoid personally. I have often worked alongside amazingly brilliant communicators with no formal education, and the trappings of certain conventions have lost meaning for me. In addition, much of what I write is stream-of-conscious, and pours out. I rarely edit those writings much. My fingers have to fly to catch up to my heart; stopping to shift keys means losing the trail. I don't want to miss any words.)

"Writing poetry is a deeply spiritual process for me: it connects me to my true Self. It brings a higher perspective to my personal story (a common theme for my poems). Whenever my heart is full—either with joy or sorrow— I turn to writing poetry. And I always feel quiet and peaceful after my heart has poured itself out into the poem."

Tara Anand

HOLDING THE FULL MOON

BY MAUREEN KWIAT MESHENBERG

a sphere,
a gyre:
spiraling deep and through forever
layers unfold layers—
the peeling back of me.
sight of your full bloom:
circular shine within,
the empty sky.
let me not return to the
circling, to what was,
what thoughts catch the atmosphere
and keep it all still and waiting:
what waits at the other end of the thread
as I bend to the light of your creating.
the stars breathe you in
with awe, and then breathe out
and scatter upon the dark edges of me.
clearly I see the path winding
but what is truly meant to be:
the wise call of the ancient ones
beckoning me to my journey,
holding the Full Moon glow
to my soul, and to surrendering.

"As women, we are constantly changing. From one day of the month to the next, our experience of the world may be completely and utterly changed--as too may be the bodies that we wade through the world from within. For womanhood, is a constant ebb and flow of cycles, of waxing and waning roles, definitions, and meanings. Our lives take on meaning through the spaces we allow to take hold of us; through the cracks of truth and calling that's deep roots burgeon on the wake of our being. Those germinating within our hearts, affirming the rich life-blood that runs feverishly through our connected frames. For we, as women, are all connected. We only need open our hearts to be."

JESSE JAMES

WHY DO I DO THIS?

BY MARIANN MARTLAND

Why do I do this? Why do I write and keep writing? Why do I sit here each day and pour my heart out onto a page that seems to know me better, to get me more than the people I have spent a lifetime hiding from?

Why do I put my heart into a string of substantial, insignificant words, when I do not even want to look at my heart, let alone allow my pen to get a full, partial or even the most minuscule of views that I sometimes only just manage to expose?

Why do I do this?

I do this so that my mind can breathe.

It has no other route for exhalation. And inhale, oh, this is where it comes to take in its first clean breaths in its crumbling world of stagnantly polluted air that is stunting its growth with every passing second of suffocation.

I do this because my soul is bleeding.

It is bleeding out all over my wounded body, forcing me to leave its stain somewhere so my bloody mess of truth can be tangibly recalled, long after neatly stitching my soul back together, cleaning away all traces of blood and leaving no scars or war wounds behind.

I do this because my soul needs to bleed.

It needs to be allowed to burst out of its sterile yet dirty prison, which gives no escape for its cravings to break and to be infected and to heal and to grow. It needs to give vision to the crimson tears which pool around its core, needing a moment to cry out blood into the white room of its captivity.

I do this for my body to release.

Untangling the tightly knotted tensions, memories, revelations that relentlessly become twisted, tethered and bound as they play to my mind and heart the knowledge, memory, emotion that my body has been gripping, weaving, forming into a solid, unbreakable mass. To allow my body to be cracked open, explored and set free.

I do this because my heart needs to create.

It needs to write a self-portrait of its ugly, heavy, life-giving pulses that cavort around its shell as I curl into the corner of my shielded, blackened, expressionless world. It needs to paint meaning to its existence, giving life to its every skipped beat and each lingering thud.

I do this so my senses remember:
To hear the inner wisdom of the universe speaking through my hands and my heart.
To see the wonder of the world in my own versions of living and loving.
To smell all of the magnificent scents and breath-taking fragrances of life and death.
To taste every morsel of sweet and sour, bitter and bland that being alive can offer.
To touch and to feel, and feel, and feel, and feel, and feel...
I do this to remain alive.

To allow myself to live and die and be reborn; to rip my life into a million tiny jagged pieces, to mend it and mold myself into who I am.

To let myself give and receive and share and to keep hold of what is rightfully mine: to throw it away and take it all back again.

To give myself time to find my life, my questions and answers, my pain and comfort, my *self* tucked away behind the mystery of past, present and future versions of my story.

I do this because I know no other way.

I know nothing but to feel through words; a written, spoken, verbalized expression of all that is good, and bad, and broken, and whole.

I know no other way to hold onto my world, than to share it and give it over to the universe when I can hold it inside no longer.

Why do I write and keep writing?

I write so I can see who I have been, so I can be, so I can become.

I write to make sense, make nonsense; so I can make.

I write because my spirit calls me here, because my spirit *is* here.

I write because it is in me, a part of me.

I write because *this* is who I am.

"I would say the most profound lesson I have learned is that it's really not very difficult to access a deeper wisdom when you enter a space of receiving a poem. Rather than trying to conjure something up, in the opening to receive the words just come. Much like with my painting, when writing poetry I am transported into a space of connection to the Divine Feminine, to my heart, my soul, and to the world and this makes me feel vital and alive. It makes me feel like I am fulfilling my purpose and making a difference in the world, and to me this is spiritual, because at the root of all that I am, I am spiritual."

Kiernan Antares

SPIRITUAL POETRY: TWIRLING AROUND THE ESSENCE

BY LAURA DEMELZA BOSMA

Cliff Of Beauty

Know we will end up in the embrace of it all.
The misunderstanding that surrounds us
is surrounded by deep understanding.
And when we end as an I
we know we are not only
in the embrace of all
we also know
we are this embrace.
Like the layers of a rose
I never left a single you
and you never left
a single part of me.
In this composition
we move through colours.
We do, we do,
we move
through fractals of petals.
Following veins, we call our own
here on this cliff of beauty I sit
just to write this poem.

The Sufi in the Rose

As a poet, I can be in all the layers of the rose, and in what surrounds it. What I love about writing poetry is this possibility to become transcendent. As in meditation, there is the inner observer, but this time she is not just sitting still. She comes out in a hand that moves to write, grabbing at the illusion and at the same time aware of how what she writes is 'passing by' and actually 'not really there.' A beautiful way for a writer to collect material is free-writing, writing without limits. Natalie Goldberg describes this technique in 'Writing Down the Bones', and also describes the connection she experiences between her practice of Zen meditation and writing. While the inner observer remains still, the thoughts keep on coming like clouds passing by. Prose writing seems to invite the clouds to appear as lively and detailed a way as possible. By describing them through the written word, they become the universe. The one thought, the one observation seems to be immensely important and all there is; why else would we take all this effort to put it on paper and draw others into it? But after writing down all that wanted to be seen and heard, all that wanted to 'pass through', I can reach the emptiness or the silence, the same way the Sufi finds the inner stillness by twirling around it.

Poetry: The Luminescent Angel

Poetry for me is not just something I do. Poetry is a way of living, all about surrendering and following my heart. Nobody just becomes a poet because it is a nice profession with secure future prospects. A poet is something that you can only be. As a child, I was a shy little mouse, always afraid to fail and fall, afraid to speak, afraid to just not fit in. But poetry came to me as some kind of luminescent angel and took me to another level of living. I suddenly found myself, in my vulnerability, being one of the most courageous persons that I had ever met. Not courageous in the sense of doing extreme sports or standing up to become a leader of speech, but doing exactly that, what I call poetry: surrendering and twirling around the essence, without being afraid of where it will bring me and what others might think about it. One of the effects of this seems to be that I do things in another order than the way they are written in books about 'how to live'.

Being courageous acquired a new meaning for me: daring to live on the edge and be terrified. While I am doing this, I find out there is no edge: there is no right way to live. Also, there is no right way of being a writer or a poet. After I had my poetry book, *Thus the Whales Fly*, published in Holland, the poetry-world was delighted. The poems were mainly about how dark and unaccepted I felt as a child, and how my imagination was there to save me, but I described these things in an almost morbid kind of way. I went to an art-academy to study 'Writing for Performance', and even though I enjoyed being able to write so much, for some reason this pattern of feeling dark and unaccepted repeated itself. I did not fit in; I had to explain myself, and it felt horrible to do so. Also, I could not socialize. Something interesting happened: as I noticed my inner voice becoming lighter and stronger, the voice that wrote, my work, was less and less accepted in the world of professional theatre and poetry. This sometimes caused an intense friction inside of me and made me feel like I was going paranoid. On the other hand, this disappointment opened my eyes to what liberated me, to do exactly that what I wanted: chanting, feeling good, dancing, yoga, poetry, falling in love, becoming a mother, starting on my path as a Doula.

I found a new balance of beauty and drama that was just right for me. Beauty could just be beauty again, and no extra drama had to be added just to make it entertaining or understandable for others. The choice I grew to have was to live a life where I wasn't being myself, which basically meant dying to me; or to live a life of beauty, of poetry, to let myself be carried by this inner voice that appeared to me as a luminescent angel.

Being Settled as the Tide Rises and Falls

My partner, Heath Thompson, who writes Taoist Poetry, went through a similar process. He tried to communicate his experience in numerous ways, but found poetry to be the most effective because of the space it leaves for the reader, in that it does not try to 'teach' something, but is more like a sharing. In the foreword of his upcoming Taoist Poetry book, "The Path That Weaves Through Clouds," he writes:

"In a way, I do not write these poems, they come to me fully formed in the same way an idea might arise to you in a light-bulb moment of inspiration. At their source is a pivotal spiritual epiphany I experienced in 2009 that totally changed my life, these pages are my way of communicating that."

Writing poetry is for Heath a daily practice that comes to him naturally. This voice of poetry is too clear to be seen as a hobby, and shows up again as a way of living. Poetry is a way to strengthen the identification with the spiritual essence and peel off old skin that does not fit anymore. That is what I see in my beloved, who, just like me, basically left the life he had behind, to come into the poetry of being. Out of inner peace, the poetic life simply arises.

She who knows
does not chase after results
realising this moment is an outcome
that naturally arose out of Itself.
To give up on wishing for one thing or another
is to be free.
Her likes and dislikes
do not disturb her settledness
they simply arise and fall
as a response to circumstance.

She neither loves the beginning
nor fears the end.
Once she realised all appearances are a single Face
she forgot herself
and wandered freely
in the empty space of Nowhere.

—Taoist Poetry

The Poetry-baby

Most of all, I see poetry from my female perspective as love, created with the same creative energy as a baby growing in the uterus. Even though from the brain we do not have the conscious knowledge to create a human being, this intelligence flows through you and me naturally. Sylvia Plath has written a beautiful, rather dramatically intense poem about this life-creating-love in her poetry book about pregnancy and birth, "Three Women". This one is spoken by the Third Voice:

"I wasn't ready. The white clouds rearing
Aside were dragging me in four directions.
I wasn't ready.
I had no reverence.
I thought I could deny the consequence -
But it was too late for that. It was too late, and the face
Went on shaping itself with love, as if I was ready."

This is also spiritual poetry, not only painting beauty, but also the dramatic, the "unwanted", the life that arises as it is, with all the human feelings that belong to this. In poetry, these "secrets" can be as they are, without judgement. Spiritual Poetry shapes itself with love.

"Writing poetry is a spiritual process for me because it allows me to hear the earth speak in her quiet, beautiful, outrageously tender whispers...in the act of listening, hearing, translating and writing I have an opportunity to connect my breath and my soul to the earth; to align my pulse to hers and to celebrate Oneness. And in all of that entirely internal, deeply personal process, poetry also becomes a vehicle to share that connection. Poetry enables me to live vulnerably in the world: To open my heart to everything."

Sally McKinnon

I BELIEVE

BY CARRIE CIULA

I believe in the lively-green leaves of deeply-rooted
dandelion.
I believe in the restorative power of a black-as-night brew of
nettle.
I believe that I can, at times, hear my feet screaming out to
touch the earth.
I believe in the innate intelligence of water.
I believe in the healing power of cuddling—and of laughter.
I believe in the calming properties of coconut ice cream.
I believe in colors— especially blues and greens.
I believe in fairies.
I believe in being naked in the company of the sun.
I believe in the inherent ability and desire in all of us to
explore love and connection. I believe that everything
happens with purpose.
I believe in keeping my mind open.
I believe that purity attracts purity.
I believe in the certainty that fireflies make all hearts smile.
I believe that I could take all of the money in our house,
make paper money airplanes, fly them off of the tallest
building and not feel regret.
I believe in kindness.
I believe that there is a fuzzy line between brilliant and
loony.
I believe in simplicity.
I believe in dancing at least thrice a day.
I believe in being still at least thrice a day.
I believe that plants recognize me and my thoughts.
I believe that words can get in the way of clear
communication.

I believe that I am in the most abundant company when I am hiking through the woods.
I believe in things that I cannot see.
I believe that we already know, yet spend much time trying to remember.
I believe in stretching and an occasional sprint.
I believe in earth-made food.
I believe good soil is essential to good living.
I believe that most things taste better with a spoonful of cinnamon.
I believe in the perfection of this process.
I believe in voting with dollars {airplane dollars;)}.
I believe that one of the greatest pains in our world is of unexpressed potential and creativity.
I believe in ripple effects.
I believe in magic.
I believe enough in the journey to keep stepping.
I believe in reinventing inventions that are no longer positively inventive.
I believe in change.
I believe in myself.
I believe in you.
I believe in us.

"My poetry reflects my most intense, raw and vulnerable side: it exposes my soul. I only write poetry when I'm deeply moved to do so. As a result, it is a process, which unfolds almost beyond my conscious will. It presents itself with an urgency and necessity, which comes from somewhere deep inside and insists on flowing out and onto the page."

FREYA WATSON

Chapter Six

Waning Gibbous Moon

"...The moonlight spells your
name when you're not looking.

You are not drowning.
One day, you will look back
and think I made it.

And you will have.
You will have."

Darshana Suresh

THE WANING GIBBOUS MOON

BY KIM BUSKALA

This is the moon of decreasing light. After the full moon the sunlit portion of the moon begins to decrease, and we are entering the waning Gibbous moon. Our thoughts turn inward as we began to digest ideas and emotions that were presented as the moon grew to full. Be it I, or we, or she, the moon has an influence on what we believe to be true. Now is the time in which writers usually become still, listen, and reflect on what it is that moves within us; that which takes us to the next stage in our lives: mirroring the changing phases of the moon. The moon is not as full in this phase: she begins to empty and our minds become open to *receive* the knowledge that accumulated as she grew to full. Through writing poetry, we sift through and find that which serves us and holds true. With the written words, we let go, release, review and renew.

In my own writing, as the moon moves from full I express a sense of completion. Words must now expose what knowledge I have gained. All I have assimilated spills forward in the coming days. For now, I will be still and allow knowledge to settle into my bones. I will become heavy with thought. Soon, it will shake loose, little by little, slowly, as I attempt to make sense of it all. It is in the writing of poems that I attempt to put one and one together and notice what needs to be exposed. This moon reveals what really matters in me. Sometimes, when this information arrives, it appears like a distant star, from another planet, a name unknown.

Suddenly the writing on the wall becomes clearer; the need to capture the meaning and write it all down is pounding heavy in my heart. Afraid as I am to cross over to another path, and leave the past behind, the remaining light of the moon assures me I will be fine. As trees do, my body and I—deeply rooted in my beliefs—have weathered many a storm: leaves have fallen, only to be reborn. Slowly, I choose to allow the winds of change to carry thoughts of yesterdays away. The need is strong for my voice to be heard, so I write, and as I do, I feel a sense of freedom and rest.

I feel so tired, having enjoyed all the abundance as the moon grew to full, and this waning moon is a time for more sleep, a time to tap into my dreams. Allowing my inner clock to rewind, as the moon recedes, as the illumination begins to dim, lessons are exposed. Writers watch for these inner messages: things that ring true, and often repeat themselves. With my imagination as my guide, I breathe it in, eat it, and write it down to digest it. Settling into the comfort of home, my soul feels soothed. Through music, a warm bath, the touch of another, I ease into a dreamlike state of being. Then my poems become as big, bold and beautiful as the moon herself, just before she hides away again, and, eventually, my words along with her.

LUNA MONTH

BY JULIA W. PRENTICE

She flits so liltingly
Across my page
Winged wonder
Skipping and weaving
Her influence touching down
Briefly, lightly
To rise up once more
Wherever she lights
Each tiny step is ink
A dash, a stroke
On that magnificent
Waiting blankness
Drinking up my soul
With her tiny beak
Spilling it back out
To rest in stanzas
On my hungry tablet
Moth to flame
Word to pen
Heart to world
Then she achingly departs
Delicately flying upward
Her patterned wings
Beating out symbols
On light-filled air
A breath later
And she is gone
Where now my muse?
On to sip sweet nectar
From another's flower
And to flit across their page
While mine stays empty

I LISTENED

BY MARGARET BEDNAR

I cannot tell you what tomorrow holds
nor what yesterday means just yet,
but I know last evening I listened

as summer's last songbird splashed
its lyrics against a tangerine sky,
its sentinel voice bowing
to river's restless murmurings
of numbered sun-drenched days.

I smiled as stubborn oak, fully ablaze,
stood defiant, prepared to hang on 'till spring
despite wind's gorging appetite

while more prudent creatures scampered
and burrowed beneath falling, spiraling
canopy, snuggling spring's promise

and I adjusted my jacket, pulled out
my mittens, and saw my breath
beneath beaver moon's filtered light.

SHE REACHED

BY LESLIE CAPLAN

Behind the windowpane, I watched the rain come down on a steel blue day. A pen in my hand and a blank page, I wrote in a stream without stopping for twelve minutes. This is what came out: a revealing of me and where I'm at these days. I often don't know what I write until I read it back. It is a channeling of sorts. The 'me' that moves out of the way so that the 'me' that is the deepest can be accessed. I loved reading this one out loud to myself. What it showed me is that I am no longer reaching for anything. I reach for reach sake and in that reach of non-reaching, I reach in and traverse the trail of gems that lead me the only place I want or need to go.

She reached down
Not for any particular reason
Just to reach somewhere
To do something
with her hand and spine
and the curve in her lower back
she reached
like a yawn
stretching mouth and jaw so open & round
she reached down
and followed a trail
of dried blossom droppings
the size of dimes
veined soft pink
curled at the edges

covering the back yard
and the carpet of her half lit room
tucked into the crevice
in the soles of her shoes
she reached
down
and gathered them up because
she didn't know what else to do
with her reaching
So she licked one
like rice paper candy it melted
into dissolve
and the floral pink penetrated
her taste buds so deep
it seeped into her bloodstream
and she fell
into a slumber of green
meadows of innocence
where the lace on her ankle
matched the color of her dress
She slipped into
bare feet
twirling into sky
a feathery lift of heart
soaring by
on the wing
of a coal-black bird sheened blue
She reached down
and picked up a thick silk ribbon that had fallen
and she tied it onto her wrist
like the ribbons on handle bars
lapping in the wind
stretching the curl into
a long, lean ripple of reaching

for the color of her deep blue mind
She chased the morning
like a butterfly
She reached
reached for hands as small as hers
as plump rose as her palms
fresh like a baby's
She reached
into memory so deep
it ingested her into its moment
where lifespan and time
dissolve
She reached
and reached
Just to reach
Not to grab hold of anything
not to grasp or yearn or get anything
Just reaching
to reach in
deep

“Writing a poem is a pure spiritual process for me. When I feel the flow of poetry it’s like a wave of light is running through me. I find myself in enlightened space, existing within the moment, merged with this creative force. And I always know when this process is finished, when all is out. Writing a poem is communication with the Soul on a most intimate level, and what comes out is always something that I’ve just integrated within me. After it’s out, I always feel that the poem introduced a theme that then comes alive in my everyday life in every detail, as if the poem needs to be embodied fully into every action, word and step that I take. It’s a very conscious, very beautiful process to me. I love these sacred moments.”

Andreja Cepus

MOTHER MOON

BY NIRVANI TEASLEY

Oh Mother Moon, who guides this inner world,
you are my secret dream, my hidden inmost need
obscured by the outer facade
that keeps me shrouded in deception.
You are the gatekeeper
of the nethermost regions of my soul.

Internal sanctums of consciousness,
Oh Luna, you are a garden for my inner child:
Vulnerable and exposed,
when your luminous light shines upon me
I am naked,
conflicted with my exoteric nature.

Oh Selene, beautiful winged Goddess!
You ride upon the intuitive waters
of my psyche,
expanding my resilience on golden wing,
clipped, I am mercurial,
quicksilver, changing from moment to moment.

Sentimental fool you take me for...
immersing me in a pool of nostalgia
only to rebirth the past,
again and again.
You slumber in the dark abyss
of my imagination, laying in wait
to reveal my aesthetic beauty.

Mother Moon, arcane enchantress,
animating the rhythmic
ebb and flow of all life.
Waxing maiden, waning crone,
wandering through my clandestine realms,
bending me to my knees, your lesson
in wholeness unravels me.
You whisper of 'new beginnings', forcing
me to bury old wounds in the
graveyard of my heart, where you stand
as guardian of my authentic Self.

THE FLOWER THAT NEVER FADES

BY JASMINE KANG

As the sunlight played with the coolness of the day, the first leaves of autumn were falling down and dancing with the wind as it was gently sweeping them away. She caught one in her hand, brushed it against my hand and looked at me. Then she gazed out into the distance. I caught her looking at a flower unchanged despise all that had changed around it. There is poetry in everything, in all beginnings and all endings, just like the fallen leaves and the flower in bloom.

In each of us there is such a flower. With time and through the experiences of life, the flower grows and unfolds itself and spreads its fragrance to the world outside. When the flower blossoms and blooms, you can see how beautiful and strong it is despise all the tests and trials it has endured. This flower will always be beautiful, no matter what it goes through, because no one can take away what it has, no one can take away its strength and beauty. That's the inner woman in you that keeps you going through all pain and sorrow, hardships and struggles that always come through every phase, just like the moon.

It was poetry that showed me this and gave me a voice to express and share. The leaves were no longer green or part of the tree, but that didn't mean it was the end. It was poetry that showed me that flowers bloom and will continue to every day, because when you see beauty and strength for what it is, wherever you look, you only see flowers blooming. It was through poetry that I learned of myself and others. The essence lies in the core of all things. That is where it starts, for all things have in them the flower that never fades. You know it by its beauty and strength. And by its voice.

YOU ARE BEAUTIFUL TONIGHT

BY RUTH CALDER MURPHY

You are beautiful tonight.
Tangling with telegraph wires
and the silhouettes of leaves,
you breeze, free across the sky,
the infinite stars fireflies in your theatricals,
harmonies for your melody.
You are beautiful tonight,
your face above the chimney pots,
clear and bright, your light milky
and your face soft as an imprint in butter.
You are beautiful tonight,
making electricity a travesty
and demanding, for the sake of decency,
that the puny competition is switched off.
You are beautiful tonight,
haloed and hallowed,
soaring free and blessing me
with moonbeam kisses
and a touch of lunacy.

FOR THOSE WHO NEED NOT APOLOGIZE A DECLARATION OF SELF & WRITING PROMPT

BY JESSE JAMES

For me, writing is a spiritual process through unfolding—an embrace of slow living and circling cycles of fluid identity. Weaving poetry and other art forms, I am allowed to show up and just be. As a chronically ill introvert, my writing is the space through which I share my true voice, as speaking has never come as easily to me. In sharing my words, I have forged new life and confidence for myself, an ability to exist and unapologetically claim space for who I am. In doing so, I have become congruent with my truths the more I practice. Writing these words, I gain a power from within them, a companion force and magic. This is where I unfurl and learn, re-weave and become. And it is the acceptance of this practice that has allowed me the strength and space to heal, to take charge within my life. This piece was inspired by the brave sharing of another fierce and beautiful soul, Isabel Abott—who, joyously, is also included in this book. This is me setting space for myself, my voice, and my truths of being. Showing up in full love and gratitude, honoring all the bits and pieces that I am.

Unapologetically, I create my own equilibrium. Following no one dogma or official decree. When forms and nuance and absolutes are out of alignment with my being, I happily reject them. Defining my own rules, and quickly shedding skins from identities that no longer fit me. For I am an unapologetically ever-evolving, changing, non-static form.

Unapologetically an emotional being. I do not ask for permission to feel; rather I am filled by the capacity of my own bold heart. Unapologetically fierce. Unapologetically assertive. I am a fiery and untamed force. Unapologetically expressive & vocal, innovative, & creative. I claim my intelligence an asset. One never dulled by the ego of someone else. Known is the value of my own mind. Unapologetically knowledgeable and wise, yet ever still learning. Reveling in the lessons from my life and others. Grounded in my own intuition and knowing, I'm not sorry for listening to and being guided by both.

Unapologetically liberated. Reclaiming the right to define every aspect of my identity for myself. Retelling my stories; taking from within the ones assigned to my body, my being, those set with the intention and purpose of doing me harm. Unapologetically, I rise beyond the hurt. I make meaning of these titles that are uniquely mine to own.

Unapologetically claiming space and healing in the word woman—when that fits—remaining myself, genderqueer. I'm not sorry for the confusion this creates. For I know how I feel in the ways I own my identity. Fluid in myself, in choosing my own name, pronouns, and titles, in healing the woman wound.

Unapologetically spiritual, but not religious. I am spiritual solely for myself, no one else.

Unapologetic for my joy, my anger, my love, my sex. For the ways in which I create, and embody and thrive. I do not apologize for showing up and being visible, just as I am.

Unapologetically a sexual being. Unapologetically sexy. I do not apologize for the extent of my experience, nor for my full enjoyment of, my active participation in, or my love of masturbation & sex. A lover of bare skin, I'm not sorry for owning my body and not shrinking to be smaller than I am. Neither am I for loving my curves, and allowing them to be both seen & enjoyed.

Unapologetically a pleasure seeker—in all aspects of life. I'm not sorry for knowing the difference between wants and needs, knowing that it's okay to go for what I want. That not all action must be taken out of necessity or survival. That it is okay to enjoy the simple luxuries I have. And to do this without internalizing guilt or shame within.

Unapologetically loud and crass and bold and profane. But also, poetic. Soft. Compassionate. Empathic. Understanding. Sometimes all of these things at once.

Unapologetically I nourish my body in the ways that I see fit. I take great enjoyment in food, and comfort. An act of service I offer to myself and others, done with no assumptions, moral hierarchy, or guilt. Unapologetically vegetarian, not a meat eater, nor vegan. I make choices based on my body's internal language, and circumstance; practicing self-care through improving quality of life. Plant-based foods are what I need, what feels good. Yet ill-health and poverty are also part of my experience. I do not apologize for either of those, nor for the choices I make to accommodate them. Pleasurable healing and culinary hedonism are forms of nourishment. Unapologetically, I eat what I enjoy.

I won't apologize for being a nurturer yet not having children. Nor for the fact that I still don't know if I ever will, or even want to yet. For knowing that is not something I have to do. Unapologetically I am pro-choice.

Unapologetically a lover, a fighter, a social justice activist. I'm not sorry that I fight to prioritize human rights, and dismantling all systemic forms of oppression. Stepping into the face of conflict, carving room for the ability to heal. I am unapologetic for the politics I keep. And for how political my personal is. Unapologetically occupying space while queer, while genderqueer, while a survivor, while poly, while femme—sometimes androgynous—while poor, while chronically ill, while disabled, while neurodivergent, while feminist. I own *all* that. All the pieces. And I love it.

Unapologetically a writer, a storyteller, an educator, and advocate. I am a hedonist creatrix, a full-spectrum birthkeeper, sexual health educator, herb wielding feminist, radical narrative healer, and dream-weaving visionary. I won't apologize for not settling into one routine, or for having so many interests—roles in which I thrive. For this is the work that moves me, empowers me, ignites me. And I don't give a damn that to some others, the value of my worth is seen as less for doing unconventional work. I know my own worth.

Unapologetically, I reject the idea that we are the sum value of what we produce for someone else. Or the wage they determine our labor is worth. As too, the idea of life having no meaning, until it is lived for someone else. Unapologetically, I fought to live this life. And now, I live for me.

I am not sorry for my resistance, my rebellion, or my defiance. All have helped me become the person that I want—that I needed to be to survive. I'm not sorry for the methods I used to drag myself beyond the violence of trauma and grief either. They saw me through and kept me hanging on. Unapologetic for acting out of necessity, and seeing myself to the other side of what was hard and broken. I'm grateful to myself for that. And, I'm not at all sorry for how long it has taken me to heal.

Unapologetically, I claim space, definitions, experiences—both the traumatic and joyous occurrences—and I do this for myself. I name names. And tell my story. And I'm not sorry that I use my voice now to write and speak out about all of the painful, discomforting things.

Unapologetically, I also claim joy. And laughter. And meaning. Sacred community, boundaries, and love. Forging all within times of difficulty and struggle, I am not sorry for returning inward and seeking balance when I find myself going numb. Unapologetically, I live in the spaces of in-betweens. And of rejecting absolutism—all the judgment and expectation that such extremes bring. Unapologetically, I dig and claw out spaces for myself and others, places where we are free to just be.

Without apology, I show up to the world with all my bits and pieces.

Unapologetically, I live as me.

When we are taught to measure self-worth based in the names, stories and values assigned to us from others, often we shrink away from our own power and truths. Ever seeking answers from external sources, surrendering in trust to our intuition and knowledge may become a burden buried, difficult to indulge. Yet, it is through communing with our spirit, in listening to our internal language, that we find heart and home to hold ourselves. Gaining agency; in claiming rights to spaces, identities, and meaning of our own. We are dismantling the internalized messages of patriarchy; those of shame and of guilt, the ones that tell us to make ourselves smaller, to seem less "too much," and more digestible; those that have us ever apologizing for our unique essential personhood.

Thankfully, in writing and in poetry, there is no need for this. The page only asks that you show up. There are no rules or pre-requisites for doing so. Only that you come as you are. In all your joy and messiness, brokenness and splendor. However you do you.

So today is for collecting all our bits of bones and spirit, all those that belong to us, that *are* us, and speaking new life into their being for ourselves. Reclaiming identity and carving out space. Knowing that it is our deserved right to practice this, without any need for apology of self. Radically rewriting our own narratives of empowerment, allowing these truths to overflow into and permeate other parts of our being beyond the page. Here are we; thrusting our words out into the blank ether with only ourselves in mind, entrusting the process of the word and form. Rebelling in a deliciously necessary act of self-indulgence and self-care. For we have awakened to the truth: that there is no need to apologize for who we are. Not ever. Reclaim your right to space! Write everything you've never been sorry for, but were taught to apologize for anyway. Write every ache and joy and ecstasy that has been long-hidden because it was "too much." Write it all. This space deserves it. And it is your right to be, you. Go now, and write!

"Unapologetically I..."
"Unapologetically a..."
"Unapologetic for..."
"Without apology I..."

PART III

Integrating

Chapter Seven

Last Quarter Moon

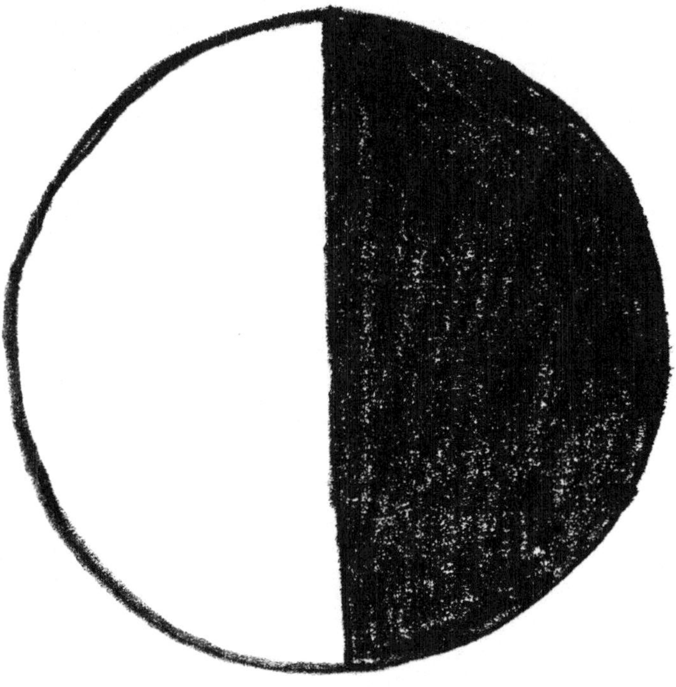

"The moon is a loyal companion. It never leaves. It's always there, watching, steadfast, knowing us in our light and dark moments, changing forever just as we do. Every day it's a different version of itself: sometimes weak and wan, sometimes strong and full of light. The moon understands what it means to be human. Uncertain. Alone. Cratered by imperfections."

TAHEREH MAFI

LAST QUARTER MOON

BY GINNY BRANNAN

"By the full moon's light our desires we know.
By the waning quarter we ebb and flow..."
—Unknown

The moon, our ever-constant companion, mysterious light in the darkness: goddess, night traveler, ruler of oceans—nearly all civilizations from ancient to modern have been captivated by you, following you, reveling in your story. Cerridwen, Luna, Artemis, Selene, known by these and so many other names. Even our Native Americans had titles for you—Wolf Moon, Snow Moon, Corn Moon, Hunter's Moon—in your cycles through the heavens ruling the months and seasons. We gaze at you from afar, shadowing you, observing your transformation as you recede past full and transition into final quarter. Though you are slowly waning, your light still shines brighter than all of the other lights in the night sky. And as you transform, so your dominance on nature evolves with you. Even the mighty oceans and seas bend to your influence: the tides slipping now to Neap phase—a time of balance, a time of least difference between high and low water. Is it any wonder that we humans—who are composed of 77% water—may be governed by your changes as well; that your lunar body may indeed play a critical role in the tides of our consciousness?

We sense your changes deep in our souls. This is a time of releasing, a time of forgiveness, a time of cleaning up: of putting everything back into place and letting go of the emotional intensity of previous weeks. During this disseminating phase the time arrives for us to reap the rewards of a job well done with celebration and accolade.

As writers, we intuitively sense these cosmic changes deep within our being. We reflect on them and are drawn to share them in our words—perhaps in the sharing to better understand the shifts and rifts, the effects of these changes inside us; or perhaps to allow us to open our hearts and minds, discovering the pathways of our own release. I know the allure, the call of your waning moon. I've felt your invitation to release the pain of the past through words that rise from deep within me. And I have found myself adrift, caught in your Neap phase: a limbo with no "high" and no "low," lost somewhere between the *ebb* and *flow*.

Oh pale-faced Huntress of Souls, we feel your command, convergence, confluence—with all of our being. You shine on the pathways of our consciousness, and in your waning light we come to understand that all things have a season, and that all that fades will again be reborn.

THE UNDERTAKING

BY GINNY BRANNAN

She views the world through autumn eyes
that on this day are cast in gray
as winter tries to tip the scale.
Weeks and months and years have passed
to leave eroded and refined
each moment lived; each bend and turn,
etched in crease and smile line.

And always playing in her mind
the words that paint the world she sees—
the people met, emotions felt;
thoughts that bend and twist within
and beg escape from their confines.

When did such purpose come about—
a want, a *need* to somehow share
and bare the colors of her soul...
when even casual observation
implores discovery on a page.

And the words.... always ruminating,
to form and re-form, while creating
background music heard by one.
You'll see her jot a line or two
on any scrap or sticky note,
or back of an envelope will do.
And on rare times when words align
to culminate with her inflection
she'll deem a poem or piece complete
or at very least well-honed

to "acceptable" perfection.
She sees her world through autumn eyes
as winter creeps up on her trail.
Time has deepened tone and voice
(so often lost within the forest
of other voices in the chorus)
becoming still as life assails...
till call to write once more prevails;
another story whispers, waiting,
the challenge in the undertaking.

THE MOON: A MUSE-IN-THE-MAKING

BY NEJOUD AL-YAGOUT

When I look at the moon I see a face. And in the dark nights of the soul, this moon—this face—reminds me that I am not alone. All I have to do is look up and connect with my cosmic companion. Through all her phases, the moon holds me in her tidal waves of energy, embracing me; and though she is not smiling, there is an inexpressible trust between the two of us, whether she is a full moon, a half-moon or a crescent. And, in her absence, she teaches me that nothing ever truly fades into oblivion. She teaches me about detachment, as well. She disappears and reappears and nobody feels pain, for we know she will be back at the right time, the right place. She teaches me that phases and cycles do not define us. The moon is always the moon, even when she is not complete: remaining a part of us, even when she is not on our minds.

More importantly, the moon has taught me about love: the kind of unconditional love that waltzes in my verse. She becomes a muse for eternity; the silent observer that teaches us about connectedness, oneness and the underlying essence that deeply connects us all—a topic I often explore in my poetry.

And though I refer to her as a she, the moon is equally a he, inviting us to a realm free of polarities, where even gender is transcended. She is a mother and a father. A teacher. And in her silence, her stillness, she invokes our admiration. Many have explored her, only to be steeped even further into her mystery. Every part of her is scrutinized, yet she welcomes all without resistance. In her wisdom, we learn that nothing is truly happening. Everything is there for the purpose of evolution of consciousness. And, when our obsession subsides, the message is clear: we are here to explore ourselves. Sometimes, it takes a rock in the heavens to wake us up from our stupor, bringing us back to our own, more essential inner exploration. It is as though the moon is telling us to look inside. Only by looking inside can we truly understand her.

Instead, we have chosen to look further outside ourselves and in such a way, that the moon—in her beauty and wisdom—proves to be a delightful distraction. We would rather focus on the moon, waxing and waning, rather than deal with our own highs and lows. We would rather focus on her craters of "imperfection," than delve deeply into the volcanoes of our own being. Perhaps her craters are whispering to us that beauty is flawed, imperfect. Maybe this makes it easier to deal with our own idiosyncrasies. Such humility!

Some have even worshipped her, but she remains humble in the expansive sky, unfazed. And so it becomes easy for me to love her.

As ever, the moon is a muse-in-the-making, for she teaches us surrender.

NOT AFRAID TO DROWN

BY MARY BACH

Poets are not afraid to drown
but I have not written
in weeks.
I know there is treasure
buried deep
but I think this time:
"Don't look!
Let the monsters sleep."

I dread the dive
so I stay at the surface
bobbing amid
the flotsam and jetsam
of meaningless platitudes
safe, bored, numb
struck dumb
in the depths of thought
where I once sought answers
but now paralyzed
when I think of the size
of the iceberg,
the depth
of the ocean.
I fear death by drowning

But what else can I do?
So I pick up my pen
take a deep
breath
and dive.

OCEANS OF WORDS

BY JULIA PRENTICE

See the lonesome poets bobbing on the surface, adrift in the ocean's waves of words. Life raft paragraphs deflated: waiting to be upended by the wave's power, sinking below the rough-tossed troughs and peaks. Fathoms deep the Marianas Trench awaiting. Diving down to a place without air or light, lungs squeezed shut so no breath can escape, barely able to think one jot or phrase as the brain starves and the pressure builds. Rising meteorically upward, towards the faint blue light, narrowly avoiding blackout, gulping in gushes of paragraphs, tomes and novellas until surface is attained. Then choking, spurting them out—those gushing, tumbling letter droplets—spraying sunward, forming fountains of words. Geysers and waterspouts carry them. They fall upon sparkling whitecaps of paper. Raining down to wet the surface—are they words or tears, brought up from those leviathan depths? Torrents of seemingly unceasing flow, ripping through soul to mind, mind to pen and pen to the waiting page...

The brain, with newfound fervor, oxygenated and empowered, coughs out lines and lines of prose, tossed and tangled into seaweed stanzas. Conch shells of conundrums and nautilus of nuances litter the sands below: to be sought like buried treasure. Searching through rocky reefs for the barnacle covered oyster volumes. Patience and pain, prying each open to reveal the radiant pearls of truth inside, yet finding only gritty dregs, to be abandoned on the wide ocean floor.

Wading through the shallows, the rivulets of words drain out towards the sea. Stepping foot upon the heated grains, mincing betwixt ancient bon mots dotted like jellyfish. Crunch of littered themes and plots underfoot, abandoned dreams. The wrack and detritus withered there reveal no unbroken shells of meaning. The dread Spanish man-o-war waits to inject poisonous ink into the pen. Then jets out blackly inside the mind, numbing it. The tumble has become trickle, the beach sands now are desert. No drops, no alphabet soup simmering, to slake the thirst for new poems. Just an aching, burning waste to be slogged through, dragged tongue-tied thought by thought. Broiling sun beating down, shriveling skin and branding the soul. Devoid of creative juice, veins brittle, blood turned to dust. The mind now full of bleached white skulls—those of published pieces—staring upward, laughing.

Giving up even hope of ever creating meaning again. Yet sun wheels through the sky— an inevitable turning, setting to usher in the full moon. Under its light, pulled by tidal swells, the soul senses moisture nearby. Drawn towards the dampness, drops of hope fall like spring rain in the mind. Eyes welded shut by heat are slowly opened. And sparkling in the distance, the next body of water is spied. Staggering, I run towards it, to quench urgent desire to write. Filling the mind with oceans of words once more.

LUNE-LOVED

BY RUTH CALDER MURPHY

I'm gazing up at you, again
—your perfect smile,
shining silver blessing on my upturned,
adoring face.

You're beautiful tonight,
shining bright,
just above the rooftops,
right there, where I can see most clearly,
shining—as it seems—for me...

I breathe my habitual prayer
to you, to galaxies,
to all celestial bodies everywhere
—my wordless prayer that rides on condensed breath
and rises like incense to disperse,
somewhere between Heaven and Earth...

I name the stars I see
—puny names, given by
little people, like me,
who play games of "I Spy"
with the night sky—
and whisper love in their direction,
wishing they were listening...

I'm gazing up at you again,
delighting in your perfect smile,
returning yours with mine,
every time you shine.

LULLABY SCRIBBLES

BY MARIANN MARTLAND

my prettiest poems,
my finest words,
often find me as i drift off to sleep.
for a second i resolve myself to finding a pen,
to scribble my soul on scraps of paper,
i know my heart will not carry
their beauty through my nightmares.
then i remember these words
are not made to be seen,
they are not for you.
they are mine,
softly rocking me through my slumber
as spoken lullabies for my mind.

SACRED LIFE BEFORE US

BY ANITA GRACE BROWN

Sacred Life Before Us.
If I should put down my phone
I might feel red-hot sizzle in my bones
Gazing at autumnal crimson

If I should put down my pinot noir
I might see melancholy behind your eyes
For all the times I neglected to

If I should put down the remote
I might hear you say
How lonesomeness metastasizes

If I should put down my fork
I might truly taste the flavor
Of sacramental union

If I should set aside my sensual novel
I might smell arousal on your flesh

Inner vibration might merge with outer
Divining a perpetual state
Of exuberance

If I should put down the shiny toys of
Distraction
I may have to contemplate
The very lie
Of my
Mortality

Having
Experienced
Holy breath
Bridging
Heaven and earth

Chapter Eight

Waning Crescent Moon

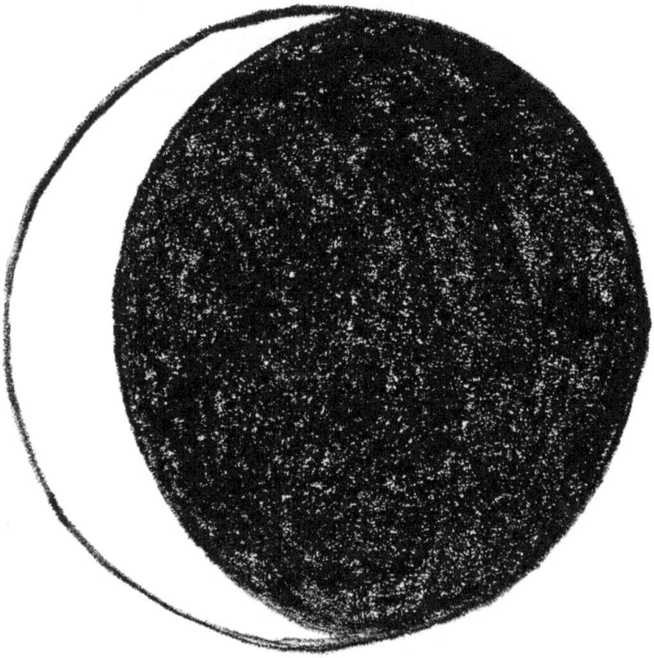

"But even when the moon looks like it's waning...it's actually never changing shape. Don't ever forget that."

Ai Yazawa

WANING CRESCENT MOON

BY TAMMY T. STONE

She is the moon on her way home.

She is flooded with the light of where she's been as she moves, with a hushed contemplative awareness, back to her refuge in the dark.

The dark—a cave, a womb, a soft space for gathering strength, for assimilating the powers gifted on her long and ripe journey as she makes her descent into the lush pre-dawn of new beginning.

She has aged, but she is Time without bounds. This is the mysterious allure of the cycle, of the opposing forces of light and dark, struggle and emergence. It is also the transcendence of duality, a wisdom that never dims but commingles with the Wisdom of Ages.

She has travelled far, unfurling like a blossom into her full naked power, and now readies to turn within. She has experienced; she has birthed, embraced and struggled; laughed, cried, despaired and loved; she has *traversed through*. She has moved the entire world with her fierceness and mercy; she has sung and wailed and reflected her secrets, as she has mirrored and absorbed the entire realm of heart's knowledge.

We see her now, a lovely, waning crescent, a sliver of refraction, mostly obscured. As the sun rises, the crescent moon fades into the power of day, but she is still moving westerly, still immersed in the flow of life and story as she makes her dip down into the horizon.

The moon in revolution; so, too, our body's breath as we experience the great joy of deep inhalation and exhalation, surrendering to the cycles of life that course through our physical, emotional and spiritual beings.

We inhale and are filled with the light of expansiveness and inspiration. Then we exhale, letting go of all that's been contained within. We release, sigh, surrender. As we near the end of our slow, sweet exhalation, we find we have to work a little bit harder to expel and release the last of what is hindering or blocking us, the obstacles buried inside. Only after this necessary and glorious release, this deep long sigh, can we come to the thrilling hinge of the complete pause, before beginning again. The waning crescent moon, this border, this last letting go.

To write as to be: it is the nature of our being, of all Being, to thrive within the joys and hardships as they go round and round, the very fabric of our (r)evolution. In our Time of the Waning Crescent Moon, we find a space of serenity amid the encroaching darkness. We gently separate from our patterns of negativity, from bursts of activity and praxis, and honor the after-light of our expression. We welcome the shadows, we seep, quiet, in our ever-growing wisdom.

The poetry is always within us. But now we wait, we breathe out, we close our eyes. We rest in our divine intuition and bow at the altar of our coming rebirth.

TALE SPINNER

BY GINNY BRANNAN

Revealed now in the waning light
I hang aloft at heaven's gate
to spin the stories of the night

With urgency the stars ignite,
the seamen's guide to correlate—
revealed now in the waning light.

The crickets chirp with rare delight;
their nocturne song reverberates
to spin the stories of the night.

Harsh landscape disappears from sight
while streetlamps burnish cityscape,
revealed now in the waning light.

Upon a park bench moth alights,
as lovers' voices iterate
to spin the stories of the night

Yet, I am but a satellite...
a drifter dressed in pale opaque—
revealed now in the waning light,
I spin the stories of the night.

"I am an owl by nature. For me, writing poems always happens in the dark hours. The Moon is part of it, my power animals are part of it, and the 'quietude' that the late and great Maya Angelou spoke of, allows Goddess, the divine creative energy, Shakti, to do her dance with my breath and words. There is definitely magic in writing poems. A-HA moments always come."

Krista Angelique Katrovas

THE WRITER IN ME

BY ISABELLE ANDRES

I was walking in the woods, introspecting about what it meant for me to be a writer, when suddenly, this poem came to me. It happened pretty much all at once, so I stopped walking, picked up my pen and the book I was reading at the time, and I let the lines write themselves in front of my eyes from the bottom of my heart. Writing poetry is rather new to me, and I was quite amazed to see what my heart had to say about what it means for me to write.

The writer in me tends to be solitary:
armed with her rucksack bag,
her pens and her note pads,
she embarks on her own adventures
never too sure of what she will find.
She wanders around the globe,
seeking new emotions, new worlds;
pursuing the new in all its allure.

The writer in me tends to be solitary:
for she travels the spaces of her mind,
attuned to the rhythms of her heart,
listening to the calling of her soul,
guided by the words of the Universe.
Carrying the heavy luggage of her past,
she forever treasures the nows,
for they are both her fate and new baggage.

The writer in me tends to be solitary:
losing herself in the labyrinth of her life,
she knows her time here is no rehearsal,
for she is there to make sense of her maze,
she is there to share what she finds.
She knows at times some doors must be shut,
so new chapters can have a chance to be written,
and her story can begin to take shape and be read.

The writer in me tends to be solitary:
she loves to lose herself within,
for her inspiration alights while she is there.
But rare are those times she is truly lonely,
for she paints new worlds with her words,
meets new faces through her chapters,
feels new emotions through her stories,
and creates magic with her ink.

The writer in me tends to be solitary:
yet, she creates her own big family on her journey.
She knows love is no matter of blood,
that all she meets hold something for her,
she knows she too has something to offer,
and that she is them and they are she,
she knows such meetings were meant to be,
and welcomes all in her heart-family.

The writer in me tends to be solitary:
yet in secret she forever dreams,
that one day her words will be read,
that one day, her stories will be shared.
Yet, in secret, she forever dreams,
That when she goes, she will forever stay,

through the bit of herself that she gave away:
subtly, yet sharply, throughout her stories.

The writer in me tends to be solitary:
but like all those who surround her,
she is also a human soul,
and there exist those odd chapters in her story,
where she feels truly lonely,
when she loses touch with her worlds,
when she can no longer find her ink,
when she fears that gloomy blank story.

It is in those odd moments of her life,
she secretly wishes for her friends,
to seek the writers within them,
to gently embrace her with their worlds,
to softly cuddle her with their words.
It is in those odd moments of her life,
she seeks refuge out of her worlds,
into the words of those who, like her,
like to call themselves writers.

THE LAND OF MYSTERIES

BY SOPHIE GREGOIRE

Life is a wave...

We need to move forward and to embrace the full rollercoaster to grow. To become who we were meant to be, to be the gift we initially received.

There is no standstill. Life progressively unfolds. Perspicacity grows. While we move along the way of days, the truth unravels. There is no settling in what's not really us.

Sometimes, unfortunately or amazingly, life takes us to the new. The heart knows, the intuition whispers, it calls. It has blown the truth for years of dawn. But the mind resists.

And the day comes when the heart wins. But there is no need of sword, no need of fight. Our within wins, naturally, as seasons dance in circle, because it trusts. And faith wins.

Faith and hopes may lead us to unknown places, lands or people. So we let go, gently, to what isn't us anymore.

Slowly we rest in the void. The vacuum in which the past has gone and where the future is still waiting behind a line. There, contemplating both what's behind and a glorified past, we gather our strengths.

And one day, we take the leap: The leap behind the line. And we move on.

There is no more, here,
To see
There is no more, here,
To breathe,
Darling.
The City of light is city of ghosts is city of sanctuaries.
One day, possibly,
When on top of the mountain of dreams
We'll be back,
Dear Country.
Country of our first walks,
Infant steps
Gently hopping,
Dear Provence.
Our untamable ocean waves
The wavy hair of the free ones,
Our first bike-rides.
Oh how much we've smiled there,
How much we've laughed
How much we've loved
Oh how Sunny France once was,
The unforgettable countryside tracks.
Oh how much we believed in living at a standstill,
When we had no wings.
How life could have been simple,
If we had no calling.
How far away
In space and time,
They now all seem.
But forever dancing in my mind,
Beauties stopped in time
My frozen statues of smiles.
The cheerful arabesques,
Of the sparkling earrings.

Of course,
Love
Still.
But need to go,
Soon,
You know.
The ways less traveled,
The unnamed paths
The leap of the traveler,
You knew.
Yes, it's a Goodbye,
To the Land of Mysteries.
But maybe some time,
In this life
Or in another shot of time,
I'll be back.
When Words spoken
Light handled
Love given
To other needing hearts,
When I have come full circle.
One day
Dear Country,
When I know why on Earth
I've come on Earth that time
With such a mind full of dreams,
I'll fall,
Once again,
For the hundredth thousandth time
Under my olive trees' stars,
Smell the set-in-stone perfume
Our first strolls.
My parents' gazes
The radiant ski slopes,

The unforgettable smiles.
And I'll rest,
Quietly
Mattress of lavenders.
Surrounded by a bunch of kids with blue eyes.
And that day,
In their bewitched looks,
I'll read
I'll find
I'll catch
Tiny sparkles of light,
The letters,
Of
Our
Whys.

TALKING MYSELF INTO ONE MORE POEM

BY TRACIE NICHOLS

(1ST THOUGHT)

The last one
wrung me
like an old
washer.

Left me
flapping
thin and
ragged
on the line.

Transparent.
Insubstantial.
Unraveling.

So I'm afraid,
dear blank page,
that the good
ones have all been
written.

You'll get
no more
wordscapes
from me.

(2ND THOUGHT)

Unless...

That wind-swooped
strand
over there.

If I can tangle
my
fingers
in
its
texture.

Follow
it
tumbling,
spitting word-scraps
tripping
sideways...

(3RD THOUGHT)

"Hello Erato!"
you tricksy
lyric lender.

Sly, slippery,
elusive muse
of mine.

Oh, but this time
you're caught.
This time
your lilting
word tumbles
are mine.

For, my dearest muse,
I'm already holding
my pen.

PULLING DOWN THE MOON

BY ISABEL ABBOTT

i sit in conversation with colleagues,
read and study and write about religious revelation.
i take notes, consider questions, know none of it as
    belonging to me.
me, the none, the not taken, the religious unwound.
but outside the ideas of right and wrong, in the place where
    freedom lives.
outside the walls that house words.
outside is the moon. forever changing, forever returning,
hidden and revealed, new and full. always whole.
and is this not the world and realm of poetry?
this hunger. this need. this stripped open offering to what
    the living do?
for whatever god is or is not, if anything at all,
there is you:
        and you're the honey and the moon.

BE STILL

BY CAROLYN RIKER

Winter's circumference translates silence. Ebony brings a blanket of comfort in the stillness until a late rising dawn. Moon, always there: A half blink of shadow, a crescent of an eyelash, opulent in fullness, spellbound in nothingness, and my true friend.

I'll gather strength in the dormancy of shortened days and deliciously longer nights. I'll fan inner light with words and music. I'll listen between an owl's talons and stark sketches of branches against a harsh world. I'll pour the sands of timelessness across the weeping sea and wipe the estuaries of overflow with eucalyptus leaves.

The waves like the moon whisper: "Healing, healing," into midnight until the first sound of feathers announces a morning song. And I'll curl around the voices that say: "Be still," knowing more answers will come.

RESILIENT POEMS FROM PRISON

BY ANITA GRACE BROWN

I happened to be "in the right place at the right time," as the old story goes. I was working as a volunteer at a women's federal prison, when I became witness to such beautiful vulnerability that it became like salve to my own broken heart.

It all began when I decided to incorporate writing into the yoga class I planned to offer the prison inmates. I had never led a writing class before, but as I had witnessed the added healing power of words, writing had naturally begun to slip into my classes.

Personally, looking back over my own poetry—written these past 5 years—I saw a thread that travelled deep into woundedness and pain, and then ultimately emerged from the shadows into the light. It was a light of shining hope for myself: one I also knew awaited others. And so began my efforts to help other women shine their own lights.

This is the story I shared with the women in prison. I then offered simple get-into-the-body practices with breath awareness and stretches. I spontaneously googled some writing prompts and used others I had experienced in workshops. Over the 4 week series, the women came to share more and more of their hearts in my classes: both in writing, as well as aloud.

It was a great privilege to intimately witness their growing trust in themselves. This experience opened me up to pain beyond my wildest imagination, and I found myself physically on my knees in one session, bowing in honor of their willingness to be vulnerable—both with me, and with each other.

The following two poems reflect a beautiful dance between the humanity and divinity alive in their souls. These women in prison—just like us—have made their own grave mistakes and are paying a dear price. I continue to be humbled by their fortitude and refusal to give up on life being a benevolent place, despite much evidence to the contrary.

May you, dear reader, sense through the following two poems, a rising curiosity within you to connect to the 'worst offenders' within your own self; exploring the transforming might of your own shadow, and the beautiful resilience of your own being to overcome anything: even the prisons of your own making.

SEASONS OF LIFE

BY TAMMIE JO

As dawn breaks over the horizon, a new day begins:
the wind whispers softly in her ears,
with snowflakes dancing before her bright eyes.
The rain kisses her tender lips,
the sun breaking upon her glowing face.
She lays upon a sea of hope. Sleeping
Shhh
For she is a baby and the world is an innocent place.

The clouds float by quietly without shape, no boundaries.

Tears of happiness drop to the ground; beings of the earth's gifts.
Laughter is heard throughout the stillness; leaving the sorrow of the world behind.

Running in a field of flowers, with the many scents tickling her nose—
without the burdens of the world, she plays.
Shhh
For I am a child, and the world grows in me.

Sunlight dances across the sky; I run the concrete jungle of the city and go no where
I inhale the air of the day but cannot breathe.
I hear the sounds, but know not where they come from.
I watch the people rushing around, headed to unknown places.
I run home at night and stare at the stars so bright in the sky
Shhh
For I am an adult now and the world is not as innocent as it once seemed.

A bright new day starts:
I sit in my comfy chair wondering where everyone went.
Loneliness comes more and more to my world.
Smiling people pass by my door as I lay in the darkness weeping silently,
for my voice has no sound and no meaning
Shhh
For I have come to the end of my life now:
waiting and welcoming death, and then,
the start of a new beginning.

BEING STRONGER FOR ME MEANS...

BY NICOLE

Striving to be great in all that I do, especially in being a mother and daughter.
Taking the good with the bad, living in the moment.
Reaching out for help, and never being afraid when I'm overwhelmed, or of the outcome of asking for help.
Opinions mattering, more especially those of my loved ones.
Never failing to see the good in myself, not letting anyone diminish that.
God; never shutting one door in my life without opening another, leaving room for positive doors to walk through.
Eagerness; to go home and show my family the new Nicole—all the self-improvements I have made!
I am stronger and more positive because a good friend of mine said: "I*t takes great strength to show weakness*." It's not how I fall that matters, but how I get back up. I am choosing to get up with grace, dignity, and newfound strength.
A line from one of my favorite songs is: "That's what I'm choosing to do: take back my life!" And after 6 years of the Federal Government having my life, it is finally over!

"Writing—be it writing poetry or prose—is a spiritual process for me. In fact, everything that I do in my journey through healing, understanding my life, and expressing my truth, is a spiritual process. For a long time I wouldn't have used the word 'spiritual'. My upbringing was extremely religious, and I battled against this religion for years, so the word 'energy' was all I could use to explain the connection I felt with the universe, and humanity. The connection I felt through writing fell into this indefinable process. Now I can see how writing is indeed a spiritual process in the role it plays in connecting me to myself, to others, and to the universe."

Mariann Martland

THE ROAD NOT OFTEN TRAVELED

BY RENEE FURLOW

in a sacred harmonious breath
i find the life of traveling the right path
there are hills, speed bumps and wrecks
but i have learned not to go too fast.
with the end result being held so high
we lose most of the meaning of life
because the traveling is more than getting by
    it's divinity itself helping you find all that is right.

COME HOME

BY MARIANN MARTLAND

You can come home now.
Don't hide under the weight of our blanket of deceit.
Come home
To rest in the comfort of your truth.
Take that journey back to your heart.
Come home.
Come home to me.

SOUL SCREAM

BY CATHERINE GHOSH

Waxing moon, waning sleep
I sift reality
through a hormonal sieve.

Swelling breasts, shrinking calm
My fringed soul
is mocked by the dawn.

Birds sing, the owls go mute
existential angst
fuels my internal disputes.

Rising orb, descending fears
my parachute rips
before courage appears.

Welcoming tangles, yet shunning the thread
Only scratchy conflict
turns with me in bed.

Dispersed pieces, fragmented light
I am slices of being
hiding from sight.

Snippets of person, scattering about
Connecting the dots
I murder my doubt.

Ambiguous identity, solid theme:
Before I start to bleed
I always hear my soul scream.

Moon wanes, sleep grows
Now I slip into the center
Where peace flows.

Chapter Nine

New Moon

"Every spark returns to darkness.
Every sound returns to silence.
Every flower returns to sleep with the earth.
The journey of the sun and moon is predictable.
But yours, is your ultimate art."

SUZY KASSEM

THE DARK MOON TO NEW MOON

BY JESSE JAMES

We are, collectively, awakened: to that of our truths, and our spirits. To our identities and our experiences, uniquely, yet connectedly our own. Whether we've been denied, or unrecognized, celebrated, or held and loved tenderly in this process; it is here that we've shown up nonetheless. We gathered our bits and pieces to uphold and extend spiritual process. And it is in this place, this book, that we've shared and gifted them unto you.

In our poems and writings, we claim our right to be and breathe, to dream, and speak our truths into existence. Doing this in precisely the ways that fit into, and create the worlds that we need: *our* worlds. Our own groups and spaces. Out of necessity, we built foundations, planted seeds of dreams, where there were none to hold or represent us previously before. We ask no one's permission in doing this for ourselves. (For we know we don't need that anyway.)

Defiantly, we rebel through our poems. In a world that asks and demands so often that we shrink and quiet ourselves to fit, we are defining our own elements. Enlisting our satisfaction as indicator of our own happiness. We revel within need, and want, and community: those we develop through embrace of sisterhood and family. We gravitate toward meaningful relationships, heart connections and soul-fire igniters: those that extend beyond the circumstance and limitation of only blood. We choose to go *big*, to build one another up beyond playing small. And know within our hearts that it is in doing so that we find our ways home.

There is no requirement or expectation within these sacred spaces; those we've staked our hearts in, clawed and dug out within earth and rock and city and clay. We built and grew them into magic for ourselves. These are where we stoke our fires.

Built within the resonance of being seen, and truly heard. Valued and loved unconditionally, for the very beings we are. We shed our former skins, noticing them without judgment, adoring them with gratitude, and embracing the insecurity and uncertainty that comes with change. We release them to the flames where they become ashes under the New Moon. We give thanks as they float away with the currents and the winds.

In flows of change, we do not cling to former identities beyond learning the lessons that were necessary, those that each form held tenderly and nourished us with from within.

Dancing solo and in circles, our shadows join us and unite; here we embody the limitless inspiration of duality—creative energy—that which extends itself to those who walk in their own power, knowing and tending to their own need. Committed to the work and healing of the woman wound.

Knowing that together, we are the same, but also words and worlds different: recognizing and celebrating those qualities that make us so. Elevating one another's spirits, championing for each other's hearts, celebrating the stories of one another—never competing. There is room for all of us to thrive. For we are one in our strength, our vulnerability, our anger, our grief, our love, sexuality, and desire. In both pain and triumph, ebb and flow, inhale and release; our hearts connect us.

We are the celebration and essence of all those who came before, came with, and came after us. Learned lessons passed down from one lineage and generation to the next. We are the ashen remnants of our ancestors and our shadows. In the gestation of darkness, we are renewed. And we are liberated, in our connection to one another and ourselves. An experience that etches itself beyond words, beyond category, feelings, or thought. We are free to be, whoever we need to be. To identify as ourselves, however that may be, through every changing moment and need. And to define for ourselves, to fend for what's ours; our rights, our passions, our feelings, our space.

We are the awakened ones, the ignited ones. And we've come with spirit and fire and anger and love, to heal and revolutionize the earth. In poem and song, tongue and cheek, in wit and sorrow and joy and seriousness. We come to the world to celebrate our gifts.

It is here, in our writing, that which we are takes form. And in the birth of our being, in the extension of our intuition and knowing, we release them into the world knowing they will be received with great love, and the propensity to build upon others hearts. And here it is, that we are at peace.

DARE ME A NEW LIFE

BY MAUREEN KWIAT MESHENBERG

Dare me a new life:
Dark New Moon swallowed by black,
only to expose the light of my beginning,
awakening me to my destiny,
to my quickening.

Dare me a new story:
Resuscitate me from my breathlessness,
not cautious or strangled by fear—
whatever brings up the old stories
I toss them to the flame.

Dare me to walk through the fire:
The dark will not hold me back,
it is there to make me find,
through instinctual rekindling—
my rise through the flame.

Dare me to be free:
New Moon beckoning me—
the renascence of me,
no longer dormant, stagnant or resisting.
I dare me to be Me.

MY MUTED VOICE

(OR THE SPACE YOU HOLD FOR ME)

BY MARIANN MARTLAND

Dear you,

I have been quiet lately, not vocally: I speak all of the time, nonsense mainly. No, I have not become truly mute, but maybe my soul has outwardly become mute.

My mind is constantly buzzing with the chatter of everything that fills my life with pain. But to speak it aloud might just be *too loud.*

I have entered somewhat of a dark night of the soul, my soul; a nightmare of kinds, which makes me never want to wake, for it is my reality.

It's not like anything has happened lately. Life is ticking on. *Lie.* I lie, don't I? Because so much has happened, but if I credit it then I must credit the other greater happenings of my life and that would be too much, too painful, too revealing. For now, anyway.

Alas, putting life into words becomes too huge of a task, though my heart longs to voice them and, no less, longs to voice them to you. Sometimes you and only you, as I know you know me.

You really *know* me.

Somehow, through all of this space and time and distance between us you see me, fully. You hear me. Even when I am not speaking I know you do.

So the nonsense, the nonsense I speak of to others, would be pointless for you, as I know it would not be worth any more than the muted version of myself I have been for us.

Yet I miss speaking to you. I miss putting my life into words for you, as sometimes it is one of my only safe spaces to make sense of it all.

But I know you understand. You always understand, which is so beautiful.

You are so beautiful.

And the way you hold space for me, oh, I have never known anything like it!

In my muted voice I do not feel I could explain just how grateful I am for this space. I will not try, for I would fail. I feel so accustomed to failing these days and I do not want to want to send *us* into that place.

For you and I, us, this, is so far from failure. It has always has been so.

This, us, you and I, is what freedom feels like. This is what expression creates, what friendship should be, what true life and love and acceptance is.

So I wait. I wait, patiently my dear (or mostly not so patiently) until my mental chatter finds a way to be voiced away from the nonsense. And it will, it always does.

For in the tiny cracks where my soul longs to break out of the silence it is you who I think of, and you with whom I want to share my voice with most.

In the meantime, I think of you often. And I hold the space we have so carefully created with as much grace as I can muster: anticipating every word, holding each one in love, feeling grateful for every part of your beautiful self, which you share with me so lovingly.

I love you my dear one, more than you will ever know.

My voice will find its way back. It's on its way already. I believe in this.

THE BOLDNESS OF ARIES

BY SOPHIE GREGOIRE

To reach places of freedom, we often have to leave the old, sometimes to make big moves or take huge steps in our personal lives. But, in March 2015, I recall that the new order was still hiding. We were on the edge, trying to find some peaceful air to breathe, in between the tension coming from the burial of the old, and the twirly energies of a newness that still had no shape.

I had reached an end, my mind and heart were almost scattered. I had been on the go, every day for endless weeks standing up for our truth and for our rights: a spiritual warrior of the winter. I had been on the move: I had leaped, for my own sake and of a blooming, awakened world.

Then, on April 7th, the pulse of Aries came to lift all of us, up, carried by a beautiful New Moon. She was, as my new life was at that time, still small, childish. Not fully real, not truly tangible. However, she said:

> *"I am coming today to comfort you. You have been struggling, but I am confirming to you today that you have made the right choices, for yourselves. You have been the committed warriors of the unknown, but please keep in mind that you fought for a good reason. You have been chosen, she whispered. Chosen to live a new life, that will eventually lead you to your highest potential. Today, dear ones, as a tool to your truest desires, I am offering you the boldness of Aries."*

As she was painting words on my heart, helped by the sparkles of her shiny pencil, I took notes. In the name of Us all, the New Moon in Aries whispered:

"It is there now
You can feel it.
It doesn't really remember our name,
who you were.
It is a magic spread,
rising from the eons,
of within.

It is a Soul work.
You feel a bit lost and wondering,
Why me, why Us?

Why am I supposed to do with the Gift?
Of being aware,
of knowing,
That I am part of it.

You are Unsure.
Something has died within,
Gone, Old Self.

Now you are something bigger,
the strength of Leaders
the commitment of Fire,
you will respect the Calling.

Those who read this
are still there,
have been through all the stages
since last September.
The doubts, the anxieties,
the sadness, anger & frustration,
the sounds of silence,
hopes taken away,

the vacuums, the waves.
You made it.
Rest, Be proud,
you have been living the Wind.

Those that read this have been brave enough,
to go beyond the line of fears.

You have not lost our way,
No.

You are about to find it.
Now, is Time to Act.

See the sword:
the sword of Light in your heart.
Take it.

Now is time
to make this,
all the efforts
blow your New Reality.

You have been elected.

The picture is blurred,
but Trust the Pencil.
On the Higher realms,
they know.

They made this happen,
They draw,
the waysto be followed by your feet.
There was a Plan,

since the beginning.
Now is Time,
to do your work.
Get started.

Surrender,
drop the Luggage
drop the controlling,

You have been elected."

POSSESSED

BY GINNY BRANNAN

Corpses of empty words and half-written poems
litter vacant halls inside my head.

The floodgates open, words careen
to slip and dissipate fast
dissolving just beyond my grasp.

    I heard the sound of hollow screams,
    as ghost-chains rattle broken dreams;
    their phantom shadows dance in ceaseless
    search for shape and form.

Yet still I write—
holding tight to scattered
thoughts on fragile pages,
as each word unlocks
the spirituous haunting
    of my soul.

SWAMPLAND ALTER AT DUSK

BY ALISE VERSELLA

Words: such small vowels and consonants strung together like rare pearls in oyster shells delicately on a thread. A spool of the soul unraveling, tongues panting, spittle spewing words. And the larynx chokes on the guttural sounds.

Pen ink blood and the wide ruled blue lines were the needles to prick my thumbs, and I stained the bitter white of the page, foregoing slumber for murder. Death to the skeletons of sentences not easily shaken from the closet of my cavernous mouth, the dancehalls between my teeth void of dancing dervishes, sing sweetly I do not. I don't like the sour taste: disdain and scorn and shadowed reveries. Always seeking out to hide away in my third eye mind where my thoughts are beasts and topple the crystal runes over the mantle.

Douse the sage in flames: cleanse me! I'm half sick of shadows, cleanse me. My dreams are muddled where that iron-gate to reality stands half-opened, I always forget to latch the lock at night. All the coyotes stumble in; they keep looking to my head to fall asleep in.

Words. Incantations. I'm casting spells in graphite and pencil shards of lead. In hopes that I'll be heard from some made up no man's god. That someone will hear these heart pound beatings beneath a pulse point in a quaking vein. Shatter me, shatter the windowpanes with the sleeting rain, wash me baptismal, the waters of sounds no words can define.

Words insignificant, words divine, lodged in my throat until the witching hour arrives and I join my trunk to the sink hole and submerge in the mud, root my toes and brace for the flood of glorious storms of words, inscribed in tree bark, inscribed in grass blades covering tombstones hidden in swampland retreats, while the ghosts bale woefully to the moon at dusk and all that are left of these words are their husks.

BELOVED COURTESAN

BY ANITA GRACE BROWN

gathering dissonant grief
as if in bridal bouquet
gallantly tossed
flick of wrist
into roar of nomad locomotive,
chugging
carting away
sorrow's enduring remnants

retreating
heaven's consort's bosom
womblike embrace
for mortal, earthen vessel

    lush, grassy tendrils tickle
    cheeks
    birthing
    cherished smiles

    all the while
    above
    alluring petitions
    ascension
    up, up, up

nuptials
amidst gaggles of geese
beholders of the vow
in cloudless, weightless
skies

solidity awakening vibration
a conjugal melding
unifying
simply softly slowing
an exquisite
betrothal

as above so below
blend me
until inquiry ceases

THE ABSOLUTE TRUTH

BY RENEE FURLOW

with every piece of me that is turned inside out
i find the best place to go where answers reside
is to be outside in.
there is no other more qualified to answer me
than, well, me.
because the truths we have deep inside ourselves
are the correct answers time after time.
and just because others try and point you in a direction
does not mean you have to give up on your intuition.
take each person and hold them high
for they are merely trying to help.
but know the absolute truth and secret to life
is to understand the answers are inside yourself.

FOR THE CALM

BY RUTH CALDER MURPHY

For the calm of the silent silver moon,
for the completeness of her cycle
—for the wax and the wane,
from fullness to emptiness to fullness again.
For the power of her tide-tugging sway
and her acceptance that Day follows Night
as night follows Day.

For the calm of the quiet mountain tops
and the perspective from their peaks
—for the panoramic peace
and the widening of skies to distant horizons.
For the perseverance of the climb and the exhilaration of the pace,
for acceptance that mountaintops and valleys
are all mine to embrace.

For the calm of the Summer harbour
and the embrace of Home
—for the knowledge that I'm never completely alone,
however far I go.
For the power of the moon-pulled, open sea
and the acceptance that storms follow calm—
and all are part of me.

For the calm of the constant Circle,
For the power of Spirit's breath,
For the Inhale of Resurrection,
For the Exhale of constant Death,
For the knowledge that Life continues,
that dying will follow birth,
For Connection, within me, of Spirit
and Fire, Air, Water and Earth.

ROOTS

BY JESSE JAMES

We as women are ever changing.
Just as the phases of the moon.

    Although we may appear
    in various forms and transition,
    we are ever present in our core,
    ever whole, even when not visible
    in cyclical essence.

From one day to the next,
our experience of the world
may be completely and utterly changed—
as too may be the bodies
that we wade through the world from within.

    For womanhood—personhood—
    is a constant ebb and flow of cycles,
    of waxing and waning roles,
    definitions, and meanings.

Our lives take on meaning
through the spaces we allow to take hold of us;
and the spaces we define for ourselves.

    Through the cracks of truth and calling
    whose deep roots burgeon on the wake of our being.
    Those germinating within our hearts,
    rooted firmly, affirming the rich life blood
    that runs feverishly through our connected frames.

We as women we are all connected.
We only need open our hearts to be.

"The psyches and souls of women also have their own cycles and seasons of doing and solitude, running and staying, being involved and being removed, questing and resting, creating and incubating, being of the world and returning to the soul-place."

Clarissa Pinkola Estes

THE GREAT LESSON OF THE MOON GODDESS

BY VRINDA AGUILERA

The cycle of our moon's phases serve to teach us an important lesson in the realm of the heart. The lesson is that of the fullness and beauty of giving and receiving. She moves through her lunar flow with the greatest of ease and regularity; seamlessly and gently undergoing her daily metamorphosis with wordless grace.

In doing so, she imparts her secret lesson: We cannot keep enfolded in our arms so many gifts without—having reached the fullness of gratitude—continue the dance and release. The time then arrives to open our arms and cast wide the net of blessings for others to receive.

Ebb and flow
Ebb and flow
Wax and wane
Wax and wane

The rhythms of the moon queen
Each day she edges a slice more towards wholeness
Wordlessly, without complaint she paints in her sphere
With poise and grace she hovers
Her eyes opening, seeing

Her journey to fullness pushes and pulls
A force that emanates on the female bodies of waters on

earth's surfaces
Echoed in the swell of waves and tides of Mother Ocean
The cycle of women's hormonal ebb and flow

Ebb and flow
Ebb and flow
Wax and wane
Wax and wane

Until our Moon Goddess reaches her full ripeness
A glistening sky pearl, jewel of the heavens
The cloudy night skies that have enfolded her
Gather their shadowy drapes and part
Revealing her cooling splendor

She glistens, shines, giving audience to us below
The living, sentient beings who drink in her beauty and wonder
Misty, cooling mother,
We offer reverence to your splendor

Then, the momentary pause of breath half held on the inhale
The inevitable exhale descends, following on its tail
For anything alive is never stagnant
Yet swims through its own cycle of dynamic evolution
The great lesson continues...

"A light here required a shadow there."

Virginia Woolf

ABOUT THE AUTHORS

Isabel Abbott is a writer, activist. corporeal artist, sanctuary in birth, sex, and death, love for the holy and hedonistic hearts.

Vrinda Aguilera lives in rural, north-central Florida with her husband and three children. She works as a Montessori primary school teacher and is a poet, intuitive energy healer, and life long practitioner of bhakti-yoga. She is passionate about supporting other's on their personal spiritual journeys and may be contacted at Vrinda.aguilera@gmail.com.

Zahra Akbarzadeh is an Iranian mother, cardiologist, fellowship in echocardiography, author of the published article: *Cosmic Music; Insight into the Theory of Love*, a certified teacher of Integral Deep Listening-Dream-yoga, who translated the book, "Ending Nightmares for Good," into Persian, and co-author with Jon Frederickson of the forthcoming book "Humility."

Sandra Marie Allagapen is originally from Mauritius but now lives in London where accountancy, healing therapies, crafts and poetry are some of the colors on the palette of her life. She dreams of spending more time in Italy one day and loves books, crystals and long summer evenings. Contact Sandra at www.empoweredheart.uk

Isabelle Andres loves to read, write, dance and has a passion for photography. Isabelle finds inspiration in Nature and contemporary art, and enjoys exploring spiritual spheres. She discovered poetry via introspective journaling and poetry has since fed her heart. Isabelle lives in England and writes a blog called *Belle's Pan Maze*.

Mary Bach is a writer, animal lover, bibliophile and general, all-around nerd. She's funny, but often her writing is not. She lives in Wisconsin with her accepting husband, blind dog and a small flock of cats. Mary collects quotes and has been published in *The Creative Nexus*, *Reflections from the Center*, and *Living with Nature*. Connect with her at mary3bach@gmail.com and her blog *In Other Words*.

Dejah Beauchamp lives in New England. Her first book of poetry, *Swan on the River: Poems of Grief and Transcendence*, will be released in September 2016.

Margaret Bednar is a mother of six. Creativity is a central theme in the household—all are artistically inclined and an open window might produce a recitation of Shakespeare, the latest Broadway tune, or a camera lens. So far, the neighbors haven't complained. Her blog is *My Poetic Journey* (margaretbednar365.blogspot.com)

Laura Demelza Bosma (1986) is a singing and painting poetess, Doula and mother of three. She follows the river of life and loves to spend time caring for her roots, just by being where she is, wherever she may be. This year her first English poetry-collection will be released. mothergoddesspoetry.blogspot.com

Ginny Brannan resides in Massachusetts with her husband, son, and two cats. Published in *The dVerse Anthology: Voices of Contemporary World Poetry*; and the two previous *Journey of the Heart* collections, she is proud and honored to be included here in this third and newest publication! Follow her at: http://insideoutpoetry.blogspot.com

Cheryl Anne Bratman lives a gentle life of prayer, presence, and poetry; silence and song. She is a lover and communicant with Heaven and Earth, and Their blessed cycles and seasons; beauties, wonders, and inhabitants.

Anita Grace Brown lives in NJ with her husband, two teenagers and golden retriever. They live by the family mantra, "Either everything is a MIRACLE or nothing is!" She enjoys keeping life simple and full of natural beauty, writing as spiritual practice, yoga, cooking and meditation. Anita Grace enjoys sharing her gifts at SmilingheartYoga.org

Jamie Burgess is a wild-hearted creative living in NC with her husband and four children. Her favorite past-times are tree-hugging and stargazing, while steadily working towards her dream of becoming a hospice nurse. She is committed to living with courage, daily, and following her heart, always.

Kim Buskala considers herself a free spirit: she flies by the seat of her pants. Kim feeds her soul by embracing family, nature and the arts. She is a writer of poetry, a dancer (guide for JourneyDance) and loves drawing (color crayons are her medium). Find her on Facebook or email her kbuskala@yahoo.com.

Leslie Caplan is a fiercely courageous heart who found her way whole through the alchemy of writing. A professional editor, writing coach and internationally published writer, Leslie brings it to real with an unwavering passion for honesty and fluidity of voice, heart and content. She can be reached at www.courageousheartinmotion.com

Carrie Ciula is a writer and devoted believer in sustainable, earth-connected living and whole-food nutrition. It is her deepest desire and joy to bring through the vibration of unconditional love and to hold space for all that divinely unfolds through each of us. Connect with Carrie through her website: carrieciula.com.

Susie Clevenger is an author, poet, and amateur photographer. She is author of the poetry collections, *Dirt Road Dreams* and *Insomnia's Ink*. Her work has been featured in *The Creative Nexus, Poetry & Prose Magazine*, and *Yellow Chair Review*. Susie resides in Houston, Texas with her husband Charlie.

Daya Dhara Devi Dasi is a 26-year old aspiring spiritual activist from California who loves to write poetry and is currently venturing into making music. Daya Dhara is passionate about women creating through different life circumstances. She finds that writing as a spiritual practice allows her to look within herself and grow into the woman she was always meant to be!

Rebecca DeLeo is a spiritual teacher, Reiki Master and counselor dedicated to the marriage of spirituality and sexuality. She journeys through the brightest heavens and darkest hells with her clients, unravels the mysteries of the feminine and is committed to awakening others to their goddesshood/godhood. Enjoy her poetry on her blog themotherofrevelation.tumblr.com, and connect with her here r.deleo@ymail.com

Amanda Dobby has always been a lover of words, literature, learning and language. She began writing during a spiritual awakening and continues to allow the words to flow from her heart and mind, as a form of healing and as an outlet for her inner fire, creativity and passion.

Shailie Dubois has a degree in Psychology. She practices Intuitive Prayer Healing, a combination of her studies in psychology, Christianity, shamanic healing, aromatherapy, artistic expression and a lifetime of dreaming. Her mission is to inspire community rooted in the service of God. She is the writer and illustrator of the children's book *Dani*.

Renee Furlow is a seasoned writer and offers spiritually-based services as the "Unique-tivity Guide" at her successful site "Catch A Falling Star" where she shares her writings and reflections. Her site is also home to the "Magic Musepirations" Zine. In addition to her short books that are already released, her soul-stirring poetic memoir is planned for release this year. www.reneefurlow.com

Catherine Ghosh is the creator and Chief Editor of the *Journey of the Heart Poetry Project* through which she inspires women to release their voices and has published two poetry anthologies. Catherine is co-founder of The Secret Yoga with her life-partner, Graham M. Schweig. She is also an artist, mother, naturalist and free spirit.

Sophie Gregoire is often found contemplating an idea or how to explain a new concept, with a notebook and pencil in hand. She is an independent soul who loves to ponder over our world and humankind. She loves writing to transform her endless thoughts into some kind of reality and traveling both faraway and deep and her heart & mind. She savors coffee, encounters, yoga and meditation, with her cat as her greatest muse.

Jennifer Hillman is a published writer/poet, certified Intuitive Life Coach/Reiki Master and shares her services and words on JenniferHillman.com and her podcast, Abstract Illusions Radio. She has two published books of poetry in the series *Embracing Souls: Poetry of the Dance* and *Words of the Heart*, available on Amazon.

Jesse James is a 25-year old disabled, genderqueer educator, activist, storyteller, & hedonist creatrix. A herb wielding feminist, and radical narrative healer; equal blends mystical, myth & science. Owner of Artemisian Artes & Urban Forest, they use their voice to promote holistic wellness, accessibility, and inclusive activism & advocacy.

Jasmine Kang is a writer from California, who also enjoys art, listening to music and being in nature. Her creative work has appeared in various projects. She is also the author of *River of Light*, an award-winning collection of prose, poetry and artwork. To know more about Jasmine, visit Moonshinegarden.com

Shannon K. Lockhart is a visionary artist, poet, mother, and healer who worked with indigenous communities and survivors of genocide in Guatemala. She has published her poetry with *Rebelle Society*, *Women's Spiritual Poetry*, and in *DoveTales*.

Darshana Mahtani is a dreamer, a lover, a giver, an optimist, a rebel, a romantic, a breaker of paradigms and stereotypes, and an aspiring novelist. She wants to change the world and find the rest of her tribe. She is part of the {R} evolution happening right now, and you're invited to join.

Mariann Martland is a writer, a seeker, a lover, a friend. She wholeheartedly believes in the universe, love, connection and strength of human spirit, even when she's overwhelmed by life (there's usually at least one moment each day when she feels overwhelmed by life). You can find her here: www.mariannmartland.com

Melissa E. Martindale is a sensitive soul. She describes the blossoming flowers that we all can become. She cares deeply for others in her life and supports them and is there for them. She likes to read; True Crime is her favorite. She often spends time with her well-loved cat Tiger Lily.

Maureen Kwiat Meshenberg relates to poetry as her passion and calling. She writes from the heart and hosts Scared Writing Circles touching and inspiring others on their journey. Maureen is author of *Seasons of the Soul: Transitions and Shifts of Life*, and her poetry can be found at the Heart's Calling Poetry Facebook page and blog.

Peggy Tabor Millin is author of *Women, Writing, and Soul-Making: Creativity and the Sacred Feminine* and *Mary's Way* and editor of the anthology, *Writing in Circle*. She is also author of *Mary's Way*. Through ClarityWorks (clarityworksonline.com), she offers women programs in the written word. She lives in Durham, NC.

Ruth Calder Murphy (Arciemme) is a British writer, artist, musician, wife and mother. She's the author of several published books and several more as yet unpublished books. She's passionate about celebrating the uniqueness of people, questioning the unquestionable and discovering new perspectives on old wonders. Find her at ruthcaldermurphy.com

Tracie Nichols is a Contemporary Alchemist, EcoAdvocate, and Teacher who simply can't stop the flood of wordscapes, which tumble out, usually at 3 a.m. by the glow of the bathroom nightlight. You can connect with her at TracieNichols.com.

Julia W. Prentice has written poetry since her teenage years. She lives in California with her soulmate and her cat. She's been an ASL interpreter and peer supporter of persons with mental health challenges. She writes like breathing: in ragged gasps, mighty shouts, half-voiced whispers. Published in the *Temptation* Anthology, and at *The Tattooed Buddha*. Her blog: rebel1955.wordpress.com

Grace Gabriella Puskas is the author of *A Message from Source*, a passionate teacher of the Healing Arts, and a writer. She shares ancient wisdoms and offers sacred Attunements ceremonies through her role as a Reiki Master Teacher, Crystal & Shamanic healer and Herbalist. It is Grace's deep love and respect for Mother Earth that forms the basis of all her work, which can be found at www.gracepuskas.moonfruit.com.

Carolyn Riker, M.A. is a teacher, writer and poet in Seattle, WA. She currently writes for several online journals

(*Rebelle Society*, *The Tattooed Buddha* and *Elephant Journal*). Her personal blog is carolynra7.wordpress.com. Carolyn leads journal writing workshops and also offers personal counseling and private tutoring. Additionally, she's completing her first collection of poetry and a children's book.

Camellia Stadts has been writing for many years but did not fall in love with poetry or creating poetry until recently after going through some of life's earthquakes. Poetry heals her heart and soul. Camellia lives in Detroit and recently graduated with a BA in English from Marygrove College. She has a son, daughter and grandson: her greatest joys. cstadts5215@yahoo.com

Tammy T. Stone is a Canadian writer currently living in Japan. In awe of life's infinite well of wonders, she loves to express her passion through her photography, Reiki practice, listening, and sewing art by hand. Her first book of poems, *Formation: Along the Ganges and Back Again*, was published in 2015.

Nirvani Teasley is a veteran Navy wife, mother of four grown children and two adorable granddaughters. She is a long time folk art painter and fabric artist. In the last two years, she has evolved from her lifelong passion for reading poetry, to writing it. She loves penning poems that emphasize the Divine Feminine.

Alise Versella is a 24-year old poet from the Jersey Shore. Always one to find beauty in the pain, Alise writes to show others they are not alone in their heartaches and that poetry is a beautiful salve to heal our deepest wounds. You can visit her at her website www.aliseversella.net

Shernaz Wadia considers writing as an inward journey. She has been published in many e-journals and anthologies. She has published her poems in *Whispers of the Soul* and another book, *Tapestry Poetry—A Fusion of Two Minds*, (an innovative form) with her poetry partner Avril Meallem.

Nejoud Al-Yagout, a Kuwaiti poet, is the author of *This is an imprint* and *Awake in the Game of Pretending*. Her work has been featured in *Women's Spiritual Poetry, The Master Shift, Best Self Magazine, Arab Times, The Divan and Global Chatter Magazine*. She is an honorary member of ALL.

Ayala Zarfjian writes a poetry blog called *A Sun Kissed Life*. She is mother to two sons, and a jewelry designer who owns her own jewelry store. As long as Ayala can remember she has loved writing and questioning her journey in the universe. Ayala interacts with a lot of different people on a regular basis and loves to listen to their stories.

Printed in Great Britain
by Amazon

28590730R00152